Stories After School

BY MADELYN PETERS OLSON

RoseDog Books
PITTSBURGH, PENNSYLVANIA 15238

RoseDog Books
585 Alpha Drive
Pittsburgh, PA 15238
Visit our website at *www.rosedogbookstore.com*

ISBN: 978-1-6495-7943-0
eISBN: 978-1-6495-7964-5

This book is lovingly dedicated
to my 6 grandchildren:

OLIVIA Z

SHELBY O

BRITTAN S

ZOEY O

AARON Z

MATTHEW S

Stories
After
School

Mrs. Olson's
Classroom

All Students Welcome

Let Me Introduce Myself....

My name is Madelyn Peters Olson and I have been teaching since the earth cooled! I don't remember a time in my life when I wanted to be anything other than a teacher. When I was very young, I lined up my dolls and stuffed animals and called them my "pupils". I utilized a small chalkboard and created worksheets for them. I ran a tight ship and maintained discipline in my classroom! I taught reading and writing, but my field of "expertise" was arithmetic.

My grandmother, my Mom's Mom, was a high school math teacher. She was the typical schoolmarm with long hair done up in a hair-bun and long skirts. I was told she was very smart.

Mom was a teacher when one-room country schools were scattered all over Iowa; she had a dozen students ranging in age from kindergarten to eighth grade. She used to tell us that she had to make one hot item daily-either hot chocolate or soup- for the students in the cold winter months. She was her own janitor. She created a booklet for each of her young charges that chronicled their journeys through learning and included amusing personal anecdotes. She presented each child with his or her booklet at their 8th-grade graduation. She kept in touch with almost all her students for years after, and they all cherished those personalized booklets. I was very proud to have Mom visit my classroom at Linn-Mar several times over the years; I always valued her opinion! I had to chuckle when, after an anatomy unit in a Health class, she asked me if I really had to say the names of the body parts out loud!

My older sister Millie was educated to be a teacher in Iowa. She had no preferences as to where she began her teaching career, so Dad spread a map of the United States on the living room floor and, with her eyes shut, he twirled Millie around and had her point her finger anywhere on that map. Her finger landed on a town called Ducor, California. A phone call later and she was hired at the Earlimart School District. She packed her bags and left Iowa. She eventually came back to Iowa and taught in the school where she had attended elementary school. Some of her students were her younger cousins.

My husband is a math teacher. He taught for 13 years at Parkersburg, Iowa, and then 25 years at Linn-Mar High School in Marion, Iowa. When we first began our teaching career, he used to say that I, as a Home-Economics teacher did the cooking and he, as a Math teacher, counted the calories! When he retired, he chose not to substitute teach at all; he said if he wanted to keep on teaching, he would much prefer having his own class and his own lesson plans than to tend someone else's students. He has never wavered from that decision. Ironically, he has had to tutor our grandchildren in math on numerous occasions, even long distance when they became college students.

Our daughter Jenni and our daughter-in-law Brenda both have their teaching degrees, although they are both working in the business sector. Our niece Kim home-schools her children in Wisconsin. Our niece Heidi teaches in Iowa and our niece Susan teaches in Ohio. Teaching is in the blood line!

As for me, I was educated at the University of Northern Iowa (UNI) from where I graduated in 1967. My chosen major was Mathematics, but when a computer glitch enrolled me in a Household Equipment class I decided to stay in the class and call it one of my electives. I enjoyed the class and the teacher so much that I changed my major to Vocational Home-Economics. After graduating with my BA, I taught for four years at a small rural school, Allison-Bristow Junior-and Senior High School, in Allison, Iowa. Following those four years I chose to become a stay-at-home Mom for our two-year-old child, Sara, eventually adding two more children to the Olson family- Jay and Jenni. (They are only 11 months apart because a good old country doctor told me that nursing a baby is a built-in birth control. He was wrong!) Seven years later, in which time I had done subbing at Parkersburg off-and-on, all three children were school-age and I was more than ready to get back to the "real world" of adults! We had to leave our home in Parkersburg in search of a location where we could both get a teaching position. My husband was hired on as a Math teacher at Linn-Mar High School in Marion, and I was hired to teach Home-Economics in the Midland School District in Wyoming, Iowa, where I taught for one year. We moved to Wyoming and Steve drove 45 minutes to and from Marion daily. The next year I, too, was hired on at Linn-Mar High School, where I first taught Home-Economics. After receiving Health Certification from ISU (Iowa State University) and an MA in Education: Reading from Marycrest International University in Davenport, Iowa, I taught Health for the remainder of my 27 years at Linn-Mar, retiring in 2006. In addition to classroom teaching, I served as a workshop and in-service presenter and I was able to supervise seven student teachers. I have been a substitute teacher at Linn-Mar High School in all the years since retirement. I still love being a teacher!

My Inspiration to Write

Matthew is our youngest grandchild of six- two from each of our three children. He was born in the summer of my retirement year. He lives across the street from us and both of his parents have full-time jobs. I have had the privilege of escorting him to swim lessons and football camps in the summer, and youth basketball games after school ever since he was knee-high to a grasshopper. Our car rides to the practice sites have been an excellent opportunity to bond.

Several years ago, when Matty was in elementary school, I was telling him about an interesting article I had once read in a Child Development textbook. It said that to have an impact on generations to come there are three things you should do:

1)   plant a tree
2)   have a child
3)   write a book

Matty was curious if, because I was "so old", I had done these three things. I told him I had not written a book. I have written hundreds of class lectures over the years , personalized papers that I had read for the funerals of two relatives and five friends, an article in the Superintendents Journal, an article in *Good Housekeeping* magazine, and in one year a graduation speech presented in front of 2000 friends and family. But I had never written a book. Matty said he thought I could do it. I said it would be "cool" someday. He said, "I think you should, Gramma." We then went on to other topics.

When Matty was in middle school he asked if I still was going to write a book. He said, "I think you should, Gramma." I said it would be "cool" someday.

Any of the thousands of students I have had the pleasure to work with over the years would undoubtedly call me a "story telling teacher". I have always learned best through analogies or examples, so that is how I have always taught. This book is a compilation of many of my stories.

"Someday" is here. There's no time like the present to make an impact on generations to come. Write, I will. If readers enjoy my stories, they have Matty to thank!

Table of Contents

Tomatoes in Abundance

1967 was a year of firsts for me.

I became a college graduate with a BA in Vocational Home-Economics.

I became a wife. My name was no longer the same as was my parents.

My husband Steve and I moved in to our first home. We didn't have a white picket fence, but we did have a garden.

I became a teacher. I had five different preps in a seven-period day.

One of the preps was for three different foods classes. My budget did not support gourmet cooking. Thank goodness, many students were willing to bring some food products from home: homegrown vegetables, farm fresh eggs, fresh milk, and apples from their orchards. As for me, I was able to contribute tomatoes because we had an abundance to contribute. In our very first garden we had planted carrots, peas, beets, lettuce and tomato seeds. Everything came up except the tomato seeds. We decided then to buy tomato plants- two dozen plants. They grew tall and sturdy, as did all the tomato seeds that finally sprouted. We harvested tomatoes from almost 50 plants!

We ate some.

My new teacher friends ate some.

Our neighbors ate some.

I took full grocery sacks of tomatoes to school.

That year my students learned to can tomatoes, make ketchup and salsa, create marinated tomato salads, make tomato pies and baked tomato slices, and cook up garden fresh tomato basil soup. They were gourmet chefs, after-all.

The next year my husband and I did not plant so many tomatoes!

The Study Hall

My first job was in a relatively small community in rural central Iowa. In addition to being hired as a Home-Economics teacher, I was also assigned to supervise a study hall for about 50 students for the first period of the day.

I had turned 21 in August of that year. One young man assigned to my study hall was 20. Paul had been held back several times over the years. It seemed awkward to have to supervise someone that was so close to my age. It didn't take long for me to notice that Paul was developing a pattern in that first period study hall. Always after the final bell had rung, he would ask to use the bathroom. He would be gone for upwards of 20 minutes each time. I just knew that he was avoiding having to study. I thought to myself, "no wonder he was held back so often- he was lazy"! Dealing with a problem like this was not part of any teacher prep class in my college experience.

I didn't want to cry "wolf" so early in my first teaching experience. I wanted to look competent and able to deal with any problem, so I decided to handle this situation in my own way. After all the other students had begun to do their homework, I tiptoed across the hall to the bathroom with the full intentions of telling Paul to get back to study hall pronto. I could hear water running and splashing around; I "chickened out" about bursting in and yelling- thank goodness. Because when Paul came back and I confronted him about what he was doing, he confided in me that his home had no indoor plumbing. He was using the school bathroom and then giving himself a quick wash-up because he didn't have the opportunity to do it before school. He had 6 siblings he helped get ready for school.... After that I realized that a teacher should never jump to conclusions.

Paul and I came to an understanding after that. I never divulged his home situation to any other student. I was so glad that a relationship was built because of what happened next in that study hall....

My desk was on a 6-inch raised platform at the front of the room with student desks facing me. A small group of students at the back of the room looked like they were up to no good. Since, as I mentioned above, disciplining was not part of my college training (thank goodness, it is today!), I had to think fast about what to do in this situation. In my mind my options were to: 1) ignore it and hope they would settle down, 2) yell from my seat of authority at the front of the room, or 3) walk back to the students and deal with the situation tactfully. I chose option number three. The minute I pushed my chair back away from the desk to get up, I also was pushing the desk forward and over the edge of the 6-inch raised platform. It not only made a loud noise when it hit the floor, it also broke the desk! The Principal came running into the study hall, assuming students had started a riot. I was very red-faced when the truth came out about what had happened. It was Paul who stood up and started the standing ovation. It was also Paul who told the Principal that the desk should never have been placed so close to the edge of the platform.

After that day, the students must have decided I was human after all. They treated me with respect, and I never had a problem monitoring a study hall after that adventure!

Shirts and Shorts

My husband Steve and I were both teachers in small schools in rural Iowa, 15 miles apart from each other. I was in a carpool with three other teachers who drove those 15 miles. Since it was my first year of teaching, I was overwhelmed with designing teaching units for my 7 different classes and completing all the paperwork required of my job. It was Steve's second year of teaching in his school and he was every bit as busy as I was.

In that era, men teachers wore dress shirts and ties to school. That meant 5 shirts weekly for Steve that required ironing. It seemed like I could never get ahead of the ironing! I mentioned that problem to my new commuter friends during one of our daily trips. One of my new friends said she knew a farmwife who was looking for ways to supplement their income and was taking in ironing for 25 cents per shirt. That price would certainly fit into our budget and would free up time for me to get schoolwork done. I contacted her immediately and was relieved when she said she would be very happy to iron Steve's shirts. She even had a next-day turn-around time! Her work was much more than satisfactory.

Growing up my Mom patched many of our clothes to get more mileage out of them. In my teen years I had two favorite summer outfits- a pair of red plaid Bermuda shorts with a matching red sleeveless shirt and a pair of black-and-white plaid Bermuda shorts with a matching black sleeveless shirt. I "loved" them so much that I was more than happy to have my Mom patch them, even if it meant she had to use old jeans material to do so. Most of the wear-and-tear was where I sat down so I couldn't see the jeans patches anyhow! When I went away to college Mom took those clothes to the Salvation Army so someone else could get some use out of them. I remember her saying once that she understood that the local Salvation Army sent clothes from one part of the state to other parts of the state so anonymity could be assured.

On one of the visits to my ironing lady, as we referred to her, one of her daughters came into the kitchen while I was there bringing in my husband's shirts. She was wearing a red sleeveless shirt and red plaid Bermuda shorts. I was just about to exclaim that I used to have an outfit just like that, and then she turned around. I saw the jeans patch on the seat of the pants. I recognized my Mom's handiwork. My feelings were mixed. I wanted to tell her that I was so thrilled that someone was getting use out of some of my clothes, but I did not want her to know that I knew her clothes came from the Salvation Army. I merely complimented her on her outfit and she said it was one of her favorites!

My Mom was right. That outfit went from eastern Iowa to central Iowa.

Recipes and Fractions

My college education had a heavy emphasis on curriculum. It did not provide courses emphasizing skills such as motivating students, disciplining students, building rapport with students and parents, or juggling the many hats worn by a teacher. If we learned any of these skills, it was because we were lucky enough to be assigned to a student teaching supervisor who really enjoyed teaching; if we were assigned a supervising teacher who was "in it" for the extra money and the time it freed up for him or her, these skills were not learned before our college graduation. Thank goodness that is not the case with college preparation classes today!

Computers weren't part of the scene yet in 1967. We teachers typed papers on a manual typewriter requiring correction paper for mistakes, we used mimeograph machines to make copies (I personally enjoyed smelling those copies), we collated our own learning packets, and we put grades in a book that provided such small spaces for scores that you almost needed a magnifying glass to interpret them later! At the quarter, the Business Education teacher became the most popular person in the building because he had adding machines that we borrowed to add up all the grades written in the tiny boxes of the grade book. The first years of teaching can be very overwhelming.

One of the skills I was not taught and was grossly lacking in was the skill to give clear, concise instructions to all levels of student abilities. I had no problem giving instructions to the average or above-average student, but my classes contained many students with learning disabilities. Charlene was one of the students who had comprehension problems.

I was teaching a Foods class and utilizing the math skills of using fractions in cooking. I instructed each student to bring their favorite chocolate cake recipe to class so we could learn how to increase or decrease the ingredient amounts to accommodate a bigger or smaller number of guests at a birthday party. I was feeling clever about the project and I was certain that all the students would understand and even enjoy the task. After modeling with one of my own recipes, I instructed the students to go to work on their own recipe. Everyone seemed to be working well and independently. Everyone except Charlene, that is. I invited her to come up to my desk for further instruction. After I used synonyms such as more or less, or bigger and smaller, I asked if she knew what making a recipe bigger or cutting a recipe in half meant. The lightbulb went off and she said, "cut the recipe in half? Oh, now I know how to do it! Can I use your scissors, please?" I knew what was coming next. I knew I had failed. She held her recipe up in front of her beaming face and very carefully cut her recipe card in half! She said, "There, I did it! Now I understand!" I didn't know if I should laugh or cry.

Yes, teaching often is an on-the-job learning experience. I don't know how else to explain it.

The Make-It-With-Wool Field Trip

In the late 60's and early 70's, homemade clothing was still quite the rage, mainly because it was cheaper than store bought clothing and the fit was so much better. One of the classes I taught at my first school was Beginning Sewing. The all-female class (back then boys took Shop classes and girls took Home-Economics classes) was composed of girls who had learned sewing in 4-H clubs, girls who didn't know which end of the needle to thread, and every ability in between. It goes without saying that some of the girls could create beautiful 2-or 3-piece outfits while some felt accomplished just completing an apron.

The American Wool Council, to promote the beauty and versatility of wool fibers, yarns, and fabrics, held a youth-centered sewing competition called "Make It with Wool" each year. (It is still going strong today, by the way) None of my students were at a point in their skills to enter the competition, not even Marilyn with six years of 4-H under her belt. The regional competition was to be held in a big city that year and I thought it would be fun to take the students to see the event. We made plans to eat at an all-you-can-eat buffet in the shopping mall in the city before we found seats at the competition, being held in a nearby large theater. We drove the 38 miles to the competition in the school van and sang or told silly jokes the whole time. The rain coming down was not going to spoil our fun!

The buffet was unique; the cost was 10 cents for each year of your age. The girls teased me that I had to pay the most because I was "old". My meal cost $2.10 while theirs cost $1.50 to $1.60 each. The food was delicious and most of the girls went back for seconds or even thirds. When everyone was sufficiently sated, I told them all to "use the bathrooms here at the mall so no one has to get up and go during the competition". When we were boarding the school van, we had to sidestep many puddles of dirty water left behind from the rain. I asked again if everyone had used the bathroom before we took off for the competition. Marilyn said, "I already went to the bathroom, but now I have to wash my leg." Everyone except Marilyn started laughing loudly; her face turned beet red when she realized what a faux pas she had made. She stammered around and said it was the mud that she needed to wash off her leg, not anything from going to the bathroom. We just kept laughing. I was hoping we would be calmed down by the time we entered the theater.

We were lucky enough to all be seated in one long row at the competition. I planted myself at the center of the row so I could better supervise all the young ladies. We were eagerly awaiting the start of the event when a matronly woman said something to my students at my left; I could not hear the conversation. I did see them pointing down the row to where I was seated. I later learned that the woman had told my students that they would have to leave because they did not have a chaperone. I may have been so "old" that my buffet meal cost more than theirs, but not so old that the matronly lady saw me as a student rather than a teacher! She was the one that turned beet red then.

We all had an enjoyable evening, clean legs and all!

Marilyn graduated high school and college and became a Home-Economics teacher in Alaska. I hope her students have brought her as much joy as did mine.

The Parent-Teacher Conference

arent-teacher conferences are a necessary part of the school setting. They provide an opportunity to track the learning of the
students while forming a sort of partnership between the
teacher and the parents. Unfortunately, the parents that you NEED to
see at these conferences are not typically the ones that show up for the
conferences. The ones that DO show up are so involved in the learning
process that they have nurtured learning into their child so well that the
parent-teacher conference ends up being an exchange of compliments.

It was my first teaching position. I had a variety of students in my 7
classes. The variation showed up in the way they dressed, in their confidence levels, in their behavior, in their ability to articulate, in their ac-
ademic prowess, and in their relationships with peers and with adults.
No two students were alike and no two could be dealt with in the same
way as the other. It was challenging to meet the needs of all learners.
Many of the skills needed to be a teacher were not taught at the college
level; emphasis was on curriculum. Teaching is really an "on the job"
learning experience!

One of the students in one of my classes was Marla. She was a good
listener in class and her eyes never strayed from center front. She always

did her homework neatly and thoroughly. Her grade was a strong A. She most certainly was not a discipline problem! However, whenever I asked her for an answer or an explanation, she always blushed. I assumed she didn't want to speak up in front of her peers for fear that her answer might be wrong. Because of this assumption I chose not to ask her as many questions as I asked more confident students.

Since this was my first teaching job and it was time to host my first parent-teacher conference, I conferred with a Science teacher whose room was across the hall from mine. He gave me some good pointers, so I felt prepared. The first parent to enter my classroom was Marla's mother. Internally I sighed relief because Marla's grade was so good, I assumed this should go well. I introduced myself to Marla's mom and proceeded to give her compliments about her daughter. Never did I expect her to say, "Marla hates you"! I stammered around and said something like "I'm so sorry if I have said or done something to Marla to make her feel that way." My brain tried to conjure up any situation that would explain why she felt that way. Finally, her mother gave me the explanation: she said I ignored her daughter and rarely called on her for answers. She was right! She was dead-on right! I explained as well as I could why I chose not to put her on the spot. I then thanked her for being so candid.

The next day, Marla was one of the first students I called on. And the next day. And the next day. Her answers were correct, and I no longer saw a blushing face.

"Assume" should not be a part of a teacher's vocabulary. Never....

The Prom Dresses

The small rural school district that offered me my first teaching position was populated with many impoverished families. They were hard-working people who didn't seem to have the opportunities to get ahead in life. Many also had large families because that meant more hands to do work on the farm.

I had also grown up on a farm so I could understand their plight. I had twin sisters who were 13 months younger than me. In small school districts the Spring prom was a big event for anyone in 10th-grade and up. Between the twins and I we had 9 prom dresses by the time we graduated from high school. In college we also had formal dresses for winter dances, so that added 6 more formals to the cache. Fifteen dresses were just hanging in our closets, each with their own story to tell.

It was prom season in that small rural school district. I overheard many girls lament that they weren't going to the big dance because they had nothing to wear. I remembered how exciting it was for the twins and me to attend our school's big dance, dressed in our finest. I checked with the twins to see if they had any plans for their gowns. Together we decided how to recycle them without making anyone feel like a charity case.

Since I was the Home-Economics teacher that first year, my classroom had a dressing room to be used in the sewing unit. I hung the 15 dresses in that room and put up a sign "Dresses for Prom. $5 donation. First come, first served." The dresses were gone that first day! The new owners were so excited and so appreciative. The parents were most grateful. No one felt like a charity case.

The night of prom my room was a busy place, full of excitement. I fixed many of the girls' hair into fancy up-dos. I purchased flowers for the girls who didn't have a date to do so for them. The girls looked amazing! The 15 dresses would each have a new story to tell.

The next year I had many girls clamoring to my classroom to see if I was going to do the same thing that I had done the year before. I wish I could have helped them, but my closet was empty with no more stories to tell....

Gretel and the Crisco Award

Her name was Gretel. Her name conjures up her image in my mind. She was short and round-shouldered while her peers stood tall. She had short hair when long hair was the fashion. Her skin was blemished when a porcelain complexion was the most important thing in a young girl's life. Her clothing was old-fashioned and worn and her skirts hung well below her knees. She was the most invisible person in the room.

Gretel was a student in my classroom. She occupied a seat near the back of the room. She was quiet and kind, respectful and unassuming. Her classmates didn't even notice she was there, but I knew that she was. She tried her personal best on every page of homework I assigned and never complained about having to do it.

That year the Crisco company furnished a trophy to be awarded to the outstanding Home-Economics students in schools across America. The criteria included scholastics, personal success, and humility. It was a coveted award and it would be awarded at an all-school assembly. The buck stopped at me to choose the winner. The girls in the Food and Nutrition classes were all their own best cheerleaders in the race to win-everyone, except Gretel that is. What can you expect when your highest grade ever was a C in the gradebook, but an A in your dreams.

I knew Gretel needed to win that award. All the other girls had won more awards than can fill a memory book. All the other girls had experienced winning. But not Gretel.

I submitted the winner's name to the Principal, and he said he refused to approve it. He said I would be the laughingstock of the whole school if I gave the award to Gretel. He told me that the other girls' parents would be up in arms because any one of their daughters should be the winner. I told him she needed to win, and I would risk the consequences. He said he would not back me up at the all-school assembly.

The awards assembly was soon to be history. It was my turn at bat, and I took my hiding place behind the podium. I questioned the sanity of my decision for the first time. I looked over the small crowded auditorium. I saw the senior girls fidgeting in their front row seats. Every senior girl except Gretel, that is. She had occupied a seat at the back of the room.

I don't remember my speech, but I will never forget the hush that followed it as I announced Gretel's name. I waited for the backlash. It did not happen. Even the senior girls in the front row looked content that none of them had won. Instead a small, hunched figure came forward in that huge auditorium. It was the longest distance of her life to the podium. Gretel was crying.

Then something happened in that filled auditorium that no one will ever forget. Gretel got a standing ovation! When parents came forward to commend me on my decision, the Principal took the credit.

Several years later I saw her aunt and she told me that Gretel was cleaning houses for a living. The aunt said that the trophy had a place of honor on the fireplace mantle in Gretel and her parents' home and that Gretel faithfully dusted it daily.

Tale #1~

Parents are teachers, too. (Just ask the parents who took on the role during the Covid-19 pandemic!) Our daughter Sara was a preschooler when I was teaching her how to tie her shoes. Our first attempts were with a cardboard cutout of a shoe complete with bright-colored laces. When we were ready to advance to a real shoe, Sara convinced me that she "could do it all by myself". I watched as she successfully tied her shoe and I said "Oh, Sara, great job! You tied your shoe right!" Her response was, "No, Mommy, that is my LEFT shoe!" I stood corrected...

Tale #2~

As preschoolers, some children have trouble with certain sounds. When our daughter Sara was exploring the world of words, she had trouble with her "t-r" sounds; she somehow came out with the "f" sound instead. That meant tree was fee, trap was fap, train was fain, treat was feat. We thought it was cute until she tried to say "truck". We then taught her the word "semi"!

Tale #3~

Our three children and three additional neighborhood children were playing in our upstairs toy room. My mom, a former one-room school-house teacher used to a roomful of kids, had come to visit. The kids were quietly sharing toys and books and I had just told Mom, "knock on wood, I hope it's this way all afternoon." I didn't even have time to knock on the wooden table when the yelling and screaming began. In record time I flew up the stairs and put on my disciplining voice and reprimanded, and threatened, and scolded the six kids about sharing and caring and getting along as friends. With sad faces, they promised they would behave the rest of the day.

When I came downstairs, I felt like I had handled my mothering role quite well. Then Mom said, "Madelyn, did you notice that when the kids were behaving, you never said a thing to them. But when they were misbehaving, you gave them attention?" She then told me the secret she used in her one-room schoolhouse: Catch kids being good! I utilized that philosophy for the rest of my teaching career.

The School Bully

My first teaching position occupied my life for four years until I resigned to stay home with our two-year old daughter. In those first four years of teaching I realized that teaching was the best career for which I could have ever studied, so after my resignation I elected to be a substitute teacher in my husband's school in the town where we lived, for one or two days a week. My best friend Janet was my back-up babysitter for those teaching days.

Dallas was a senior in high school. He was built like a football player but didn't join the team because he did not like the discipline and commitment that being on the football team required. Besides, Dallas had a "team" of his own consisting of boys that worshipped the very ground he walked on. He was an egotist who was tough and verbally abusive to students because he knew his "team" would laugh at his antics and make him look intimidating. It was safer to be Dallas's "friend" than to be his enemy and become the receiver of his cruelty. He was one tough cookie, a future penitentiary inmate (my opinion)!

That day the Superintendent had called me at home to see if I could substitute in the Government class. I relayed to him that I had a cake to decorate (I decorated cakes as a sideline job to make extra money for our little family), and I hadn't had a shower yet, and I wasn't certain I could get a babysitter. He must have been desperate because he said that if I could come in, he would teach the first class of the day until I got there, and he would pay me for the whole day! Now, I love a challenge; challenges are very motivating. Within an hour I had completed the decorated cake, took a shower, fixed my hair, and procured Janet as a babysitter.

I arrived at the High-School during passing time between the first and second period classes. As I rushed down the sidewalk to the building, I could see through the glass front doors that Dallas and his entourage were pulling homework out of other students' textbooks and shredding it! His team was laughing and encouraging him. Dallas spotted me and ran to the doors. Naive me, I thought he might actually have some social skills and that he was going to open the door for me. I was wrong! Instead, he put his foot in front of the door to block my entrance. At first, I chose to be assertive and asked him to "please let me in". He laughed and so did his cronies. I increased the assertiveness and said, "Dallas. Let. Me. In." He sneered and said something very derogatory. I increased my assertiveness to a low aggressiveness and said again "Dallas. Let. Me. In. Now!" He was still sneering when he said "Ooohh, I'm scared". With his left hand he opened the door just enough to allow me to slither in sideways; in his right hand was a mittful of shredded paper which he held over my hair. The hair I had just taken time to fix- a girl's crown in glory, something you don't mess with. I said "Dallas. Don't. Do. That. I am warning you!" He must have liked challenges, too, because he released that whole handful of shredded paper on my head. I now was at full aggressiveness. I grabbed him by the collar and his waist and unceremoniously hauled him down to the Superintendent's office, his feet never touching the ground. I threw him to the floor, put my high-heeled foot on his chest, and said "EITHER HE GOES, OR

I GO. Do you understand?" The Superintendent had a hard time stifling a laugh as he said he understood. Dallas was expelled.

The first class I taught after that incident was seniors. They all just stared at me. Everyone had seen what just went down in the hallway. My heart was still beating rapidly. I broke the awkwardness by asking if anyone had anything to say. After all, I was a female and I had embarrassed one of their peers, even if he was the biggest male bully on campus. After what seemed like a long hush to me, a student at the back of the room stood up and started clapping. Then the whole class stood up and applauded. Standing ovations are amazing!

Several years after that, I learned of Dallas's new address. He is getting free room and board, free clothing, and has a toilet in his one-room cell.

"Ten Little Fingers"
Nursery Rhyme

Our first child, Sara, was born with an extra finger on each hand, off to the sides of her pinkie fingers. The genetic condition is called polydactyl. All sorts of crazy questions go through a new parents' head: is it on my partners lineage because no one in my family has extra fingers or toes? how will we get gloves for her to wear? how will we be able to protect her from gawkers and rude people? Fortunately getting rid of the "embarrassment" was a simple procedure. The doctor put a tight thread around each of the extra fingers and time caused the lack of oxygen to make the extra appendages "die", then they were literally cut off. One of her fingers has a smooth scar, and one has a tiny bump. We left the hospital on the fourth day after her birth and had an unspoken agreement to not advertise about the extra digits. The evening we brought our beautiful baby home was a planned potluck at the school to socialize before the start of the school year. My husband, the proud new father, was carrying Sara around for all to see. Another teacher's wife had given birth a few days before our big event, so that teacher was also doing a show-and-tell. When the two dads reached each other while making rounds, they were comparing the little girls to each other. I saw my husband hold Sara's hand up to the other father to examine, and then I saw the other new father hold his baby's hand up to show my husband. Would you believe the only two new babies in that room were both born with 2 extra fingers!

Sara was never bothered by her unique condition, and in fact, she wore it like a badge of honor. When she was in elementary school, she used her fingers as a show-and-tell contribution. When she was a Freshman in college, we got a phone call from a young woman asking if Sara was really born with extra digits. When I said, "she surely was" we could hear her yelling, "Sara's not kidding!" and then the phone went dead. Sara was comfortable in her own skin.

By the way, we learned early up that the polydactyl condition had appeared on both sides of our families two generations back. When our other two children were born, we counted their ten little fingers and ten little toes.

Cinnamon Rolls
and a New Job

"C hristmas City" is the affectionate title of the city where we lived for one year. The massive amount of decorations that are displayed during the holiday are breath-takingly beautiful. In the one year we lived in that tiny little town and I taught in the High School, we got to be part of those beautiful festivities. Sadly, there really wasn't much else there for entertainment for the kids to enjoy for the rest of the year because there were 3 taverns and one grocery store in the town, and that was it!

Prior to moving to the "Christmas City", I had been an at-home mother for seven years and now that our youngest two were entering kindergarten, I decided to pursue a full-time teaching position again. My husband had been hired as a Math teacher in one of the fastest growing school districts in the state. The Home-Economics job in "Christmas City" became my newest post. Our schools were 45 minutes apart from each other. That was in 1978, an era when Vocational Home-Economics teachers in small rural areas still did the required summer "home visits".

The home visits gave me an opportunity to meet my future students and their parents in the home setting, and then design curriculum around their needs. I was welcomed into a variety of homes- from modern homes to homes that may or may not have been cleaned on a regular basis to shanties that certainly were not. I remember coming away from one such home with a wet skirt from sitting on a urine-soaked couch! One house had its own junk yard filled with old refrigerators and pop cans; inside the house the kitchen floor had a hole that was large enough for a small child to fall through. Whatever the condition of the homes, though, I met some really wonderful families, too many working so very hard just to put bread on the table. My new job was going to be a real challenge!

Early in the Fall, a student named Marsha brought me a homemade cinnamon roll that had obviously not fallen through the hole in her kitchen floor. Marsha was beaming with pride; she said she had used the recipe she learned in our cooking class and that all her many brothers and sisters had loved them. I praised her talents and thanked her for saving one for me. I started to put it off to the side of my desk when she said, "aren't you going to eat it now?" I casually offered some flimsy excuse about still feeling full after eating breakfast and that I had brushed my teeth and didn't want sugar on them. Her smile turned upside down and she said "please, please try it". I knew then that she NEEDED me to try her creation. I took a small bite. It was delicious! Her smile turned right side up and she said, "you are the only one of my teachers who tried the cinnamon roll, Mrs. Olson." She walked out of the room with pride. I had tears in my eyes.

A Home-Economics position was opening up for the following year at the high school where my husband had been teaching for one year; procuring that position would mean that he would not have to drive 45 minutes, one way, to get to work each day and we could then move to a bigger city with more opportunities for our three children.

That year there were more prospective teachers than there were teaching job openings; I was one of 37 applicants for the Home-Economics position. Telephone interviews weeded out 25 of the candidates and I was fortunate enough to be in the remaining 12. I was the last of the 12 to have my in-person interview. Besides the typical interviewing questions, the Principal told me that he was going to ask a few unusual questions and that I should answer them with my first thoughts. The first unusual question he asked was "what if a student brought you food and you didn't know how sanitary their kitchen was- would you eat it?" First, I laughed to myself. Then I proceeded to tell him that I had had that exact circumstance happen to me at my last school and that I did eat the food because the student NEEDED me to eat it....

Marsha was responsible for me getting the position at the same school as my husband's position, where I would spend the next 27 years. I hope she is still baking cinnamon rolls for her own family. I also hope there is not a hole in her kitchen floor, big enough for a child to fall through.

Mmmm, Chocolate Pudding

Foods classrooms are notorious for being one of the most used rooms in a school building, particularly in a small school district. In addition to being a place of learning, the Foods classroom also is a gathering place for staff before school on days someone brings treats, or the place food is prepared before sporting events or concerts and plays. The refrigerators and microwaves are the calling card. Many school employees heat up their lunches, sometimes even during class time. Since it was my first, and eventually only year at this school, I had mixed feelings about this being a popular gathering place.

Students enjoy enrolling in Foods classes because they not only learn cooking skills, but they also get to eat their creations. They are almost always successful, but their eyes are typically bigger than their stomachs, so leftovers are a reality. Often, the students are so proud of their creations that they want to share the extra food with some of their favorite teachers or even their peers in other classrooms, during the class time. I always allowed this because it was a form of advertising for the class, it gave the students instant feedback about their cooking skills, and no food went to waste- only to the waist!

My Foods classroom was booked in every period of the school day. I taught in six of the eight periods, and another teacher held classes there in the other two periods. That meant that I needed a place to be during my prep periods; the Library was the logical place to go to because it was located right across the hall and I didn't have to carry all the papers I was working on a great distance. It gave me an opportunity to get to know the librarian very well, and we became friends.

One day my students were making homemade chocolate pudding. A kitchen team composed of 5 males had put their pudding in 6 pudding dishes. They asked if they could share the extra serving with the librarian. Their request surprised me because the librarian had her hands so full in her room that she often had to be quite firm with students, so she wasn't usually a teacher with whom they normally shared. Typically, their choice was a coach. I was pleased with their request, so encouraged them to take it to her then. Only four of the boys left, and they were laughing. I should have figured then that something strange was happening. The fifth team member quietly told me something for which he did not want to be blamed; the other boys had put Ex-Lax, a chocolate flavored laxative, into that sixth bowl of pudding!

I was not pleased. While the four boys were still in the Library, I used my room phone to call the Principal and share what had happened; together we hatched a plan. The boys came back with the empty pudding plate and began doing the paperwork required of all labs and finishing the kitchen clean-up. The Principal came in my room and asked if I could keep an eye on the library for a little while because the librarian had just experienced severe stomach cramps and had to go home. I said I would be glad to. The Principal then left the room. (This was part of the hatched plan.) I jokingly said to the boys, "Gosh, I hope it wasn't that smooth looking pudding you made that made her get sick! Did it taste fine to you?" Immediately the confessions came out. I rambled on that sometimes a person's stomach needed to be pumped at the hospital, or that the severe diarrhea it could cause might make her very sick. The boys weren't laughing any more. They said they didn't mean to have the librarian be hurt, they just thought it was funny. They wanted to know what discipline the Principal might give them when he found out: would they be expelled? would they be kicked off the football team? I asked what THEY thought would be a reasonable consequence. They talked it over and concluded that they would all write her an apology and send her some flowers. I said I liked their ideas, but I also suggested they write an explanation of their choice to the Principal and to the school board. They agreed to all the terms. I never once had to yell at those young men and they lost no respect for me in the process.

An occurrence like this never happened again.

Cheerleading Camp

When a teacher signs a contract, there might be a short clause embedded in the document that reads, "all other duties as assigned". Often those other duties include hallway monitoring or lunchroom supervision. In some schools there is an expectation that you sponsor a youth group or cheerleading squad. I was assigned the latter in my first year at a school that was one of the fastest growing school districts in the state. I knew no skills associated with being a cheerleader. None whatsoever!

Even before the ink was dry on my contract, I learned that I would be escorting five varsity cheerleaders to a summer cheerleading camp in the northwest part of the state, a mere five-hour drive away! Most chaperones from other school districts had left their charges at the youth camp on Monday with the intentions of picking them back up on Friday. The few of us who had driven a great distance stayed the whole week and we were assigned cabins big enough to accommodate up to 12 people. My cheerleading squad and four girls from another school district shared a cabin full of bunk beds and one cot; I was the token adult chaperone. The cot was mine.

The first night after a full day of hard practice, I assumed the girls would be so dog-tired that they would fall to sleep quickly. I underestimated the stamina of teenagers. They shared the usual camp stories of my youth- funny ones and scary ones. At some point when I thought the girls would be winding down, we heard yelling outside. We listened carefully and overheard enough to realize that some local boys had infiltrated the camp housing 150 girls and were probably "up to no good." That quieted the scary storytelling, pronto. Before long we heard a scratching sound on the wall across the room from my cot. A girl who we nicknamed Barbara because of her remarkable resemblance to Barbra Streisand, was on the top bunkbed by the window. Barbara went temporarily speechless with fear but kept pointing to something she spotted outside the window. We kept asking what she saw, but no decipherable sound could come out of her mouth because of the fear! Another student said "Mrs. Olson, check it out for us." I replied, "not on your life, I'm just as afraid as you are." The whole group finally guilt-tripped me into checking out the situation. I leaned Barbara's bunkbed ladder against the window, noticing as I climbed up how terrified she looked as she pointed at a location outside our cabin. It was difficult to see in the dim light outside, but I quickly spotted a harmless looking young man standing under a tree, grinning and waving at me! I relayed what I saw to the girls in my charge, but Barbara kept pointing at something outside that had obviously traumatized her. I looked outside again, saw the young man still waving and grinning, and then I realized that there was a second young man immediately on the other side of our window, his fingers spread as he pressed his hand against the glass. I had been looking between his fingers at the other young man some distance away! I screamed. They screamed. And it wasn't for ice cream! Almost immediately the camp coordinator came running to our cabin, caught the young rascals, and then planted himself outside of our cabin door with a shotgun for the whole night. We slept semi-well.

The next day was another day of hard practice. We had just settled down for the night when a tornado siren went off. We had to run to a designated safe place, a farmhouse with a basement about a half mile away. All 150 girls and 12 adults fought tree branches and pebbles and fear as we ran through the darkness to the safe place. A tornado did touch down within 15 miles of our location, but we came out of the situation unscathed. We slept semi-well that night.

The third evening we were treated to a fun-filled evening of riding a Ferris wheel and Roller Coasters at a nearby amusement park. The time spent on each ride was lengthened by the carnival workers because the facility was open only to the members of the cheerleading camp for the evening. The girls were having a wonderful evening of fun after a hard day of work. I was having fun, too, until I got on a ride that went around and around at great speed. I started to feel sick (I have been known to get motion sick) when I could feel the contraption slowing-thank goodness! It did not stop, however. Instead it reversed direction and speeded up again. Going backwards at great speed when you already feel nauseous aggravates the sick feeling! The operator must have read my green face and he quickly brought the ride to a halt. At least I made it to a nearby bush to relieve myself of the camp meal we had eaten before departing for the amusement park. I was no longer amused. The girls slept well that night. Me? Not so much.

Friday finally arrived. It seemed like Monday was weeks ago. As we were all packing to go home, the girls from my cabin presented me with a bright red shirt with a large "S" embossed on the front. They said it stood for Superwoman.

That evening, at home in my own bed, I slept very well.

Tale #4~

I've always enjoyed using nonsense words. Flapdoodle. Hogwash. Humbug. Malarkey. Poppycock. Razzmatazz. Those words are so much more politically correct than swearing in the classroom. I even affectionately called some students and my grandchildren young whippersnappers and flute-snoots! If you say any of these words with a matching non-verbal, you don't even have to explain the meaning of the term. One of my favorites was "horse's-patoot"; I used to tell my students to be kind and caring to each other rather than to be a horse's-patoot. They got the meaning! Several years after one of my students had graduated college and started a job in Missouri, she called to say hello. She said "Mrs. Olson, I discovered that horse's-patoots don't just reside in Iowa. We have some here in Missouri, too!"

Tale #5~

I was fulfilling one of my obligations, the dreaded lunchroom supervision; it often made me think of the song "Who Let the Dogs Out" by Baha Men! A 9th-grade girl was sitting alone at a table in the lunchroom.

She had beautiful, curly hair. I went up to her, mainly for the sake of conversation, and told her how beautiful her hair was and how jealous I was because I had to pay big bucks for perms every three months. She thanked me, shyly. That 9th-grader grew up to be an elementary teacher in our district. At one of the mentor-mentee workshops I was facilitating, I mentioned that students like to be noticed and that a genuine compliment was one way to show it. My former student raised her hand and said "Mrs. Olson, when I first started high school, I hated my curly hair. You came up to me in the lunchroom, bounced my curls up and down and told me that I had beautiful hair. That made all the difference in my attitude after that!" I had forgotten ever saying that, and she will always remember that I did.

Tale #6~

A teacher friend named Joel and I team-taught teachers in our district in a for-credit class based on Madeline Hunter theories. As part of the class, Joel and I took turns accompanying the teacher-students, individually, to a designated classroom of a master teacher. The intent was to have the teacher-student observe the experienced teacher and look for examples of the theories we were studying; the experience was dubbed a "Walk Through". A teacher-student named Scott went with me on a Walk-Through to observe in a Kindergarten class. The kindergarten teacher was reading a story to her pupils when one little girl in the back of the room approached the teacher and whispered in her ear, "I love you, Mrs.

M". The teacher didn't miss a beat as she rubbed the little girls back, whispered that she loved her, too, and kept on reading to the group. I turned to Scott with a pouty face and said, "I don't know how to label that one, but I can tell you that it never happens in my High-School classroom!"

Tale #7~

I had a legally blind student in one section of the health class "Perspectives on Life". GWAEA (Grant Wood Area Educational Agency) had furnished him with a braille typewriter to take notes in class. The agency also produced braille pictures that the young man could "feel" as he learned. In the female anatomy unit, he used his fingers to "see", and loudly announced, "so that's what a vagina feels like!" Every boy in the room wanted to "see" it, too.

Tale #8~

Madeline Hunter was a popular American educator who developed some innovative models for teaching and learning. My school district was one of many districts that were going to incorporate her model into our district's curriculum. She was appearing at a civic center in Cedar Rapids that accommodated the several hundred teachers in the Cedar Rapids/Marion area. My friend Katie and I marched right down front to have the best seats in the house; we were too young to know any better! The front row gave us opportunity to see Madeline Hunter up close and friendly. It also gave me proximity to approach her after the presentation and stammer out that we shared the same front name! Afterwards I felt foolish because I was probably more impressed than she was....

Tale #9~

One of my Child Development classes was about to begin when a student named Chrystal came in sobbing and talking incoherently. We deciphered that someone had stolen her purse in the lunchroom. Chrystal was being raised with four other siblings by her widowed mother, so losing the contents of her purse was an especially big deal! I had another student escort the sobbing Chrystal to the main office to report the theft. While the two girls were out of the classroom, I shared with the rest of the class why this theft was truly devastating. One young man at the back of the room stood up, walked to the front of the room, emptied his pockets of all the money he had on him and said, "I want to help". One by one, everyone who could afford to do so, did the same thing. By the time Chrystal came back down to the classroom, she was over $50 richer. Her purse was never found, but she found a lot of new friends.

Tale #10~

I taught a Health II class and one of the units was on death and dying. Most of my students had never been to a funeral. One of the local funeral homes had graciously allowed us to take a field trip there and the director shared with us the behind the scenes activity that occurs when someone dies. We were able to glance into the embalming room and to see the crematorium; we were shown jewelry that can hold the ashes of a loved one; we visited the casket sales room and decided that a casket costs about the same as a car! The students had all their questions answered in a comfortable setting.

Two weeks later, one of those students lost her brother in a tragic car accident. The funeral home we had visited was serving the family. When I went to the visitation, my student told me she was so glad she had gone on that field trip because now she knew what was going on and she could help comfort her family.

Tale #11~

I have spent more time in dentist offices over the years than most people I know; I have very soft teeth, so I lose fillings often. I have a bridge and two partials; all four front teeth are artificial caps. I tease the dentist that he should name one of his rooms after me. It could be worse- George Washington had wooden teeth! One day I was presenting information in class when one of my front teeth decided it had held in there long enough. I must have been talking with my hands and arms because when the incisor parted company from my gums I somehow flipped it and sent it flying to the desktop of a young man in the front row. Scottie very casually said, "Ah... Mrs. Olson..... I think this is yours." I have lost all four of those front teeth, one at a time, over the years, but never quite so dramatically as I did in front of the whole class!

Tale #12~

At the end of each semester I had all my students write at least two "things I have learned in my life so far" statements and then I compiled them into a booklet that each student received on our final day together. Submissions included funny things like "I have learned that you should never put your tongue on a frozen pipe", or "I have learned I'm in trouble when my Mom uses my first <u>and</u> my middle name". Sometimes students wrote things that they may have thought, but never articulated, like "I have learned that the reason my mom yells at me is because she loves me and cares about me."

One of the young men in my class was killed in a car accident a few weeks after the end of the semester. When I went to the funeral home for the visitation, it was natural that his Mom was having a difficult time accepting the loss of her son. She regretted that she had yelled at him so often but had not told him that he was loved so very much; she wondered if he even knew. I handed her one of the class booklets that I had intentionally brought for her and turned to the page where his entry appeared. "I have learned that the reason my mom yells at me is because she loves me and cares about me."

Tale #13~

After I broke an ankle and returned to school in a wheelchair, I was presenting information to my students using the overhead projector. Evidently, I was presenting faster than they could take notes because one young man got up, wheeled me into the hallway and said, "I'll come get you when we have caught up!"

Tale #14~

I believe boys like compliments as much as girls do but receive less of them. One afternoon a young man came into my room and I noticed he had a new haircut -the clean hairline is always an indicator. I said I liked his new haircut! He said, "you know, Mrs. Olson, you are the first one to notice it all day" I was glad I had taken the time to say something about it.

Tale #15~

After twice failing the required health class "Perspectives on Life", I volunteered to tutor Shane after school; when he said he couldn't stay after school because he had to ride the bus home, I offered to drive him home so that we could have work time. He agreed, and after three weeks of after-school struggles, he finally passed the class. That was in his sophomore year. After that year, I saw Shane now and then during passing times in the hallway. He always acknowledged me with a nod of the head and I always smiled at him. One morning in his senior year, Shane washed his truck, filled it with gas, closed his garage door, and took his own life. He was found eight hours later by his parents when they came home from work. A guidance counselor and I learned later that Shane had written a seven-page letter as he was dying. Most of the contents of the letter were for his family and girlfriend. One section said that the only two teachers who really cared about him were his guidance counselor and me.

Tale #16~

Because my husband and I were teachers in the same building, our three children each had us as a teacher. That made it awkward for them when it came to what to call us in front of the class- Mom or Dad? Mr. Olson? Mrs. Olson? In one section of Health, both Jay and Jenni were on my roster, and the room was populated with all their friends, many of whom had been in our home. The teens solved the dilemma of what to call me. The whole class called me "Mom".

Tale #17~

Our son Jay had a school friend that resembled him so much that we called him "Jay #2". Jay #2 was at our home on numerous occasions and always brought laughter with him. His actions always reminded me of Red Skelton, a wonderful television comedian of my youth. I remember him looking very much like the comedian one time in particular: we had a short wooden fence bordering the front sidewalk. My folks were visiting and my Dad was sitting in the living room in front of the picture window; Jay #2 knew he was there, so he pretended to fall over the fence because he couldn't lift his leg high enough to get over it; he repeated the antics enough times that my Dad was laughing and laughing when Jay #2 came dragging himself into the house and said "man, I didn't think I was <u>ever</u> going to make it in this house today!"

Jay #2 also pretended a bag of powdered sugar I was using for frosting was cocaine and he would take a big whiff of it. One day the whiff went up his nose and then the joke was on him!

Jay #2 knew his grandparent's neighbor very well from all the times he visited their home, so when the neighbor died, he wanted to pay his respects. His Mom was working and could not escort him to the visitation and Jay #2 had never been to a funeral home, so he was understandably nervous about going alone and seeing a "dead body". I volunteered to take him to the visitation. The teacher in me gave him a crash course on funeral etiquette and protocol. I emphasized that laughter and joking would probably not be appropriate behavior. Jay #2 walked in the viewing room with dignity, and then he fainted. No one had told him that the deceased had an identical twin who lived out of state and she was standing at the head of her sister's casket!

Tale #18~

When our son Jay was in 4th-grade, his test scores indicated that he would benefit from becoming involved in the TAG (Talented and Gifted) program. As teachers, my husband and I were quite excited for him. TAG met once a week for half of a day. Jay was very excited, too- at first. We noticed his enthusiasm waning after several weeks and asked him what was happening. His response was, "it's not fun to be smart". Upon investigation we learned that his regular classroom teacher didn't understand that TAG was an enrichment program that replaced some of his class work. Instead, she had been making him stay in from recess to make up the work he missed when he was gone those half days. He was being penalized for being in the program. My husband and I let Jay decide what he wanted to do; he chose to not be in TAG. As teachers we had to hide our disappointment; as parents, we completely understood his choice.

Tale #19~

Our children were in Elementary school; they arrived home around 3:00. My husband and I taught at the High School which let out at 3:30. Typically I used the crockpot for the main course of our evening meals, but one food item the family enjoyed was a turkey loaf- half white meat and half brown meat; the loaf took an hour to bake. I asked our daughter Jenni, who was 8 at the time, if she would like to be the chef that night. I allayed her fear of failure by writing a step-by-step instruction sheet and then modeling it for her. She felt confident.

When Jenni arrived home from school, she completed the instruction sheet, one step at a time: 1) wash hands, 2) get turkey loaf from the freezer, 3) take covering off the turkey, 4) put turkey in oven, and 5) turn oven on to 350 degrees. I'm sure she felt accomplished!

When we got home. The turkey smelled wonderful. The three kids helped fix vegetables and mashed potatoes. When everything was ready to eat, I asked the kids to set the table in the dining room. Jenni said she had a surprise for us. We went to the dining room and there was a finely set table- plates, silverware, napkins, and glasses of milk which had been poured almost an hour earlier!

Tale #20~

I was teaching a Sewing class. Of the 17 students in the class, five were foreign exchange students with limited English, three more were special needs students who had difficulties with hand/eye coordination, eight females had a wide range of sewing experience, and one student was a male. We had 15 sewing machines in the sewing room. It was a busy classroom!

The token male, Javon, opted to make a 5-piece camouflage outfit for the hunting season. It was an ambitious under-taking but he assured me he was up to the task. He did not disappoint me and, in fact, was quite a good role model for all the girls in the class. His perseverance and work ethics were note-worthy. That's why it surprised me when I saw Javon with his chair tipped back and his feet on the counter! I said "Javon, what are you doing??" He said he was following directions. I had to see what he meant, as did many of the interested girls in the vicinity. He showed us the sewing guide for his massive project and right there in the middle of the guide it said, "put your feet up and relax; have a cup of coffee".

I certainly couldn't fault him for his actions. I did laugh, however, when he asked me when I was going to get him a cup of coffee!

Tale #21~

Our daughter Jenni was in middle-school and she and I were shopping at a local grocery store. When it was time to purchase our selections, I noticed that one of my high-school students had just arrived at his cash register, so we decided to go through his check-out lane. My students and my children rarely heard me use swear words, so Jenni was shocked to hear me say, "Well Hello, Asshole." The cashier knew right away why I called him that name. At breaktime he and his buddies were altering their nametags and he had forgotten to remove the playful sticker that covered his real name. His nametag read "Hello. My name is Asshole". He said he was glad I noticed it before the manager did. Jenni started breathing again.

Tale #22~

Some words used by teens are of interest for short periods of time, like fads. Words like cool, deep, groovy, hippie, and mod all ran the gamut. A student came in my room and said I was really "phat". Of course, I thought he was saying "fat". I was offended, hurt, mad, and embarrassed.

I must have said "thanks, I guess" in a sarcastic manner because he quickly explained that phat was a compliment that meant the same as cool, deep, groovy, hippie, and mod!

Tale #23~

I was administering a lengthy test in Health class. The test was multiple-choice (or as some students referred to it, multiple guess) and the students were working in pairs of their choice. I encouraged kids to get comfortable, so when two of my best-thinking students asked if they could work in the hall where it was quiet, I gave them permission. I circulated during the test mainly to make sure each member of the pair was a contributing member. When I went out to the hallway, I realized that the two students out there had accidentally been given a copy with answers written in the margins. I quickly replaced their test packet, and after I had explained why that was necessary, they said, "We saw those answers but didn't know who had written them there and we didn't know if they were right, so we just ignored them." I'm sure they had!

Tale #24~

Gingerbread houses are fun for all age kids. I volunteered to bring a house to decorate for each of two boys in the high-school autism room. One of the boys was a very large kid, but a man of few words. The other boy was a smaller kid, but a man of many words, some of which weren't always appropriate for the classroom setting. I talked them through the decorating of their gingerbread houses when the smaller boy of the two said, "Oh, sorry, Mrs. Olson, sorry!" I thought he was referring to the frosting mess he was making. I said that making a mess was part of the fun and that he shouldn't feel sorry about that. He said (and I quote), "No, s-sorry Mrs. Olson. I just had a fart!"

Tale #25~

Every teacher has students that really warm their heart. Mitch was one of those students for me. That's why when he asked if I could sew something for him, I agreed. He didn't tell me ahead of time that it was a pair of boxers and that I was to sew the crotch opening shut! He intended to wear them over sweatpants, which was the fashion statement at that time. He knew his Mom wouldn't agree with the fashion statement so he couldn't ask her to do it. He also didn't tell me that he had washed them just before he brought them to my house and that he didn't have time to put them in the drier before his Mom got home. So, Mitch handed me his wet boxers and left. The things teachers do for their favorites!

Tale #26~

I had a sophomore student named Thomas who was a big fan of the Gothic look. He wore a spiked dog collar around his neck, black fingernail polish, black eyeshadow, a Mohawk hairdo, and an entirely black outfit every day at school. He was a gentle person in the classroom and caused no disturbances. But he also had no desire to get good grades; I was concerned that a poor final project and a failing final exam would mean that he would not pass the class. He needed to pass the class for graduation. I asked his guidance counselor to set up a meeting with all his teachers and his parents.

Thomas and I were the first two to show up for the meeting. He had on a light blue Oxford shirt, no black eyeshadow or painted black fingernails, and his hair was combed in a preppy fashion. I told him that he certainly "cleaned up nicely" and that he looked so handsome. He thanked me. When his Mom entered the room, I told her the same thing about his appearance. She looked at him and then at me and shrugged her shoulders, as if what I had said was strange.

Thomas came in my classroom later that morning for our class. He wore a spiked dog collar around his neck, black fingernail polish, black eyeshadow, a Mohawk hairdo, and an entirely black outfit. I commented on how different he looked from that early morning meeting. He said he always changes clothes after he gets to school because his Mom would kill him if she knew he dressed like that at school. Then I understood the puzzled look on his Mom's face when I had said "he cleans up nice".

Tale #27~

In the last week of classes I would have my students write a letter to their future child, to be presented to him or her on their 16th birthday. The letters described what high school was like, their activities, their friends, information about their parents (the 16-year-olds grandparents), their plans for a career, what they thought their life would be like, what they thought their parenting skills would be, and included pictures. I asked the students to put the letters in a safe place so they would not get lost over time. For the last several years I have been hearing from former students and the "letter" and have even received pictures of their 16-year-old reading about their parent's youth. The information is priceless!

The Cookie Bribe

I was a retired teacher, and I was substitute teaching in a BD (Behavioral Disorder) classroom for one full week. The teacher had warned me in her daily lesson plans that the six boys in her charge could be a handful, so the week was undeniably going to seem longer than five days.

I noticed that food stations were utilized in the classroom and the boys helped themselves to chips and fruit and toast and candy and smoothies all day. The paraprofessional assigned to the BD room told me on the side that these students were on the free or reduced lunch program at school, and that many of them didn't get breakfast at home because their parents or guardians couldn't afford to put food on their table. Food was obviously important to them, so I decided that bribing them with food might be a good plan.

I made a pact with all six of the boys: if they had no discipline problems in any of their classes in the week I was there, I would bring a dozen homemade sugar cookies and frosting for each one who had great discipline reports, and each of them could decorate their own cookies and take them home to share with their families.

Bribery can be effective! They were "good as gold" the whole week. All six of them. On Friday I brought in all the materials they would need, the one dozen cookies per boy and multiple bags full of colored frosting. I demonstrated how to frost the cookies without breaking them, and then showed them how to use the frosting bags to make patterns or flowers or "whatever their little heart desired". I have never seen boys who were typically displaying undesirable behavior and swearing, be so gentle and so thrilled and so on-task as those boys were as they decorated their very own cookies. When they were done with and very pleased with their plateful of cookies, they asked what to do with the leftover frosting. I knew I didn't want to take it home after they had been squeezing the bags and licking their fingers! I told them to just throw the bags in the trash can. "No, mam" one young man said. "We're going to eat it!" And they did. Those rough, tough boys looked very cute with frosting all over their faces! What a week.

The Bicycle Brain

As a student I always learned the best and retained the most information when my teacher would give multiple examples or relevant analogies. I facetiously used to think that I must have been born in Missouri- the "show me" state.

As a teacher I am aware that there are several different learning styles and that the one-stop-shopping technique does not apply to all students. When I teach, I design a variety of activities, but still have heavy emphasis on story telling. I do need to make sure that my students know when I have gone off on a tangent for the sake of an analogy, though. I explain it by having them imagine they are having a conversation with a friend when a bicycle goes by. A person's first reaction is to turn his head to see if he knows the bicyclist. When you refocus your attention to your friend you may have to ask, "what were we talking about?" In every class, most of the students knows exactly what I am talking about because they, too, often have "bicycles" go by.

After the students know the concept of the "bicycle brain", I use the statement often in my teaching. I will say, "Oops- a bicycle just went by!" when I have an example or analogy to help them understand a concept we are learning at the time. For some reason, I have almost 100% attention when that happens! (Kids like stories). Some students often refer to a bicycle going through their mind, too. A little bit of levity goes a long way in establishing rapport in the classroom.

In the state of Iowa an annual event called RAGBRAI occurs in the last week of July. RAGBRAI stands for Registers-Annual-Great-Bicycle-Ride-Across-Iowa, sponsored by The Des Moines Register newspaper. Thousands of riders from around the world traverse the state of Iowa from the Missouri River on the west to the Mississippi River on the east. I remember that the year we lived in "Christmas City" our town was one of the many that the bicyclists traveled through; the sound of the gears shifting on thousands of bikes sounded like locusts descending on the town! It is always quite an event!

Back to the classroom. One day I was explaining a concept and I alerted the students that a bicycle was going by. One example led to another example, to another, to another, to another. One young adult at the center of the room said, "Mrs. Olson, I think RAGBRAI just went through your mind!!

I hope I never tire (get it?) of my bicycle brain.

Everybody Loved CJ

Over my teaching career, I have had many special needs students with learning disabilities and several students who were "handi*capable*", not handi*capped*. The latter group included students with temporary disabilities that required crutches and wheel chairs, and students with permanent disabilities like the hearing impaired with hearing devices that required me to wear a tiny microphone around my neck to have direct access to them, a blind student who utilized a braille typewriter and braille handouts, and a student with cerebral palsy.

CJ had cerebral palsy since birth. He came from a very supportive and loving family. His parents became Boy Scout leaders so they could help their three sons with camping experiences. Other than his physical limitations, CJ was a "normal" fun-loving young man. His independent mode of transportation was a small wheelchair, but he required being maneuvered when he had to change positions. His older brothers helped him navigate the school hallways when they could. He was a good thinker and listener, but sometimes because of the effect of cerebral palsy on his muscles, he had spastic movements and difficulty articulating. But everybody loved CJ!

CJ was a mascot for the football team. He was the only unsuited member of the team that was allowed on the sidelines during games. He loved watching the games from his vantage point. That year the football team was so good that they made it to the playoffs. Unfortunately for CJ the playoff games were held at the indoor football stadium at UNI where the only people who could be on the playing field were dressed football players and coaches. All other observers were in risers with no space for a little wheelchair to maneuver. CJ's brother Charlie knew that CJ would not see much of the action in a stationery seat so he hoisted him up onto his shoulders and ran back and forth during the whole game so he could be part of the action. All the onlookers were impressed with the gesture and with the huge smile on CJ's face. Everybody loved CJ.

I was fortunate to have CJ in two classes in his senior year; he was enrolled in the Child Development class and in a class called Family Living. In the Child Development class, which conducted an on-site pre-school, he interacted with the three- and four-year old preschoolers so well that the children often wanted to ride on his little wheelchair with him! The little people, as we called the preschoolers, could often understand CJ's speech better than the big people, who were his peers. I was very pleased to have the young man in two classes that semester and I know he felt comfortable and safe in our room.

One afternoon in a different class than the two CJ had on his roster, my students and I heard what sounded like scratching on our metal door. I paused briefly and waited for someone to come through the door. No one did, so I started the oral instructions for a project the students were going to tackle when we heard the scratching again, louder. Then we heard someone say, "Help. Help. Help Me. Mrs. Olson. Help.". We all recognized CJ's voice and a few boys instantly ran to the door. They pushed it open and found CJ laying belly-down on the carpeted floor, holding himself up with his bloodied arms, with no little wheelchair in sight. That young man was fighting-mad as well as being physically hurt from dragging himself down a long hallway that spanned the distance between the boys' bathroom and my room. We eventually learned that some underclassmen thought it would be amusing to spread soap all over the bathroom floor so that other guys would slip and fall. CJ didn't notice the soap in time and his wheelchair skidded and toppled him to the floor. He said he yelled but no one could hear him, and no one came to his rescue. He said he knew where our classroom was and that I could help him, so he crawled commando-style all the way to get there. My whole class was furious and didn't think the underclassmen's antic was funny at all. Some of the students retrieved the little wheelchair and cleaned it off. Some of them found a janitor and helped him mop the bathroom floor. Some cleaned the blood off CJ's arms. Everyone comforted him. Everybody loved CJ.

It was the Spring of his senior year, 1992, and graduation ceremonies were to be held in downtown Cedar Rapids at a large civic center. The school maintenance crew had created a ramp to be used by CJ so he could wheel across the elevated stage and receive his diploma in front of 2000 people, just like the rest of his classmates. In the past years the graduation speaker was always a dynamic inspirational speaker who was so good that she could command a large speaker fee. That year she was still grieving the loss of family members who had recently been killed in a small airplane crash, so she had to cancel any graduation speaking engagements on her calendar. Rather than trying to locate another guest speaker, the senior class officers and the Principal decided to have a staff member do the honors. The senior class voted on who they would like to speak at the ceremony and my name became "Commencement Speaker".

My youngest daughter Jenni had just finished her first year of college at UNI and was already home for the summer, so I put her to work taking a picture of each of the seniors, all 200 of them. I had very little time to prepare the speech and no monetary incentive to do so. In fact, the speech ended up costing me money because I had to have all the pictures developed and I rented a rear- view projector to display the pictures, one at a time, as part of my presentation. My speech was based on the letters in the word F-R-I-E-N-D-S with a story that began with each letter. The D gave me the opportunity to tell the story of CJ at the UNI-<u>D</u>ome with his <u>d</u>evoted brother; I said their story made me think of the Boys Town, Nebraska, motto, "He's not heavy, he's my brother..." After the speech the pictures were all flashed one at a time on the screen while the song "That's what Friends are For", by Dionne Warwick, was played through the loud speaker system. I made sure the picture of CJ in his little wheelchair was the last one displayed so his image would last longer in everyone's mind. It ended up being a real tear-jerker; I didn't see a dry eye in the room, mine included.

Yup, everybody loved CJ.

Making Lasting Remember-ies

M any classes require that students memorize lists or concepts. Students always seem to know the colors of the rainbow because of ROYGBIV, and the names of the Great Lakes because of the word HOMES. Many classes require memorization, but memorizing is not easy for all students.

A memory assist that I learned at an inspiring workshop was called the "Memory Frameworks", and I chose to incorporate it into my classroom curriculum. The gist of the tool was that students would first memorize ten specific words that rhymed with the numbers one through ten: One, bun; Two, shoe; Three, tree; Four, door; Five, hive; Six, sticks; Seven, heaven; Eight, gate; Nine, line; Ten, hen.

After memorizing the words, students had to visualize each of the rhyming words; the funnier the image they would choose, the more likely they were to remember it. For example, the image for "shoe" might be a golf shoe, a tennis shoe, a clog, a heel, or even the shoe from the nursery rhyme about the woman who lived in one. Once the images are conjured up, that is a person's own permanent framework on which they can now "hang" any list of ten words or concepts.

I always gave the students a list of 10 unrelated items prior to teaching the framework. They look at the list for 30 seconds and then they write as many of the words as they can remember. Very seldom does someone remember all ten, so I would proceed to teach them the frameworks. Then I showed them a list of 10 unrelated words, one at a time. The first word in the list is imaged with the first word of their personal framework. For instance, if "dog" is the first word on the list to be memorized, then the student images a dog and their already-imaged bun together: perhaps the dog is in a hotdog bun, or eating a hamburger bun, or biting a person's "bun". No two people will have the same image. Then they progress through the list. The second word would be associated with whatever shoe they imaged, the third word with the tree, and so forth. They would name the list of 10 words by the name of whatever is at number one- in this case, the Dog list.

After instruction, 100% of the students have memorized all 10 words! Weeks after that instruction, the "Dog list" appears on a quiz, and it always amazes the students that the Memory Frameworks works!

Well, our daughter Jenni was on Spring break from her first year in college and came to my classroom for a visit; it had been more than five years since she had learned the "Dog" list in Child Development, and that happened to be the lesson in our class that day. Talk about a coincidence! Jenni said, "I know the Dog list!" The students hounded her to say it. She had 100% retention.

Memory Frameworks really works.

Parenting: It's NOT ALL it's Cracked Up to Be

In Math and Science classes, students immerse themselves in and practice their new skills with immediate feedback. Child Development classes give students an opportunity to learn parenting skills; the best way to learn about parenting would be to give each student a baby with whom they could practice the new skills. That will never be an accepted strategy in high-schools; parents and school boards would certainly frown on such a suggestion!

Since sometime in the late '90's, school districts have invested in "Baby Think it Over" and "Real Care Baby" infant simulators that look like real infants; they require feeding, burping, and diapering, and they cry at random times in the day. The infant has a bottle, clothes, and a car seat! They give today's Child Development students a taste of reality for a time period ranging from one day to a weekend or even for one week.

I started teaching Child Development in the 80's when the infant simulators weren't on the scene yet. The only two options for giving my students a tiny taste of parenting experience was either to furnish them with a 5-pound bag of flour to carry around, or to give them an egg-baby to carry around. I chose the latter for economic reasons. I partially boiled the eggs in shades of pink and blue, and had my students draw a small piece of paper from a toy stroller; the paper had a color and a number on it, representing the sex and number of babies to which they were assigned. One young gal was assigned triplets, and several new parents had twins. The students were to carry the baby(s) with them for one full week; if they needed a babysitter, they had to pay 25 cents per hour to the sitter, and the sitter had to verify in writing that they had been paid. If the baby was dropped and cracked, they were charged with child abuse and had to plan a funeral. They all were required to keep a detailed journal.

Very few students left the egg-baby unadorned. Most students furnished a little baby bed with little covers and painted faces on the egg; some students even cut off pieces of their own hair and glued them on their baby. The really caring student-parent provided the egg-baby with mobiles and toys and miniature bottles. It was a fun week for everyone involved!

There was an away-football game the first evening of the project. A student bus took students to the game, and I was a chaperone on the bus. The football players were on a separate bus. It was rewarding to see many of my students with their "newborns" on the bus. One of the football players was in the Child Development class and I just assumed that he would get a babysitter on that first night. We were watching the game when I spotted an egg-baby on the players bench with the new father sitting next to it. At a point in the game when there was quite a commotion going on in the end zone, all the bench warmers, including the new father, jumped up and started to run in that direction. Suddenly my student reversed his direction, ran back and picked up his baby egg, and then headed back to the end zone. I jumped to my feet and clapped; I think everyone in the stadium heard me yell, "Now THAT boy gets an "A" on this project!"

As for the young girl who was assigned the triplets- she grew up, graduated from college, got married and gave birth to twins. She called me and laughingly said that I was to blame!

The Superintendent and the Experiment

Teachers regularly attend summer classes and workshops to stay up-dated with current "best practices". During the school year, in-service training offers one-or two-day workshops for teachers with similar curriculum needs. Some of the in-service trainings were very helpful and even inspiring; some, sadly, were a waste of time.

One of the more inspiring workshops I attended had a lot of hands-on activities. We participants were all paired off with "someone outside of your curriculum area". I was paired with Dr. P, our new Superintendent who had just strolled in to see how the workshop was going. Each pair was then asked to share with our partner "a frustration you currently have in your classroom". I shared with Dr. P that I really enjoyed teaching the sophomore required-to-graduate Health class, but that many of my students were "hormones on tennis shoes" and difficult to keep focused. Dr. P shared with me that he had recently completed a course led by a man named David Langford who had taught the participants about his "Quality Tools" which helped learners to be their best advocate and that facilitated team learning and helped with problem solving. Dr. P was frustrated because he had all this new knowledge, but no classroom in which to test it.

The workshop facilitator then had each pair brainstorm ideas for helping each other with the frustration they had, and then formulate a plan of action. A lightbulb appeared over Dr. P's head and he asked if I would consider allowing him to team-teach the students in one of six sections of a health class called "Perspectives on Life". I liked the idea, but had a few reservations: would my students feel comfortable sharing opinions on sensitive health topics if the Superintendent was in the room; what would other teachers think about my teaching abilities if the Superintendent was in my room every day? I thought about it for all of two seconds and jumped on the opportunity!

Dr. P and I met in my classroom, outside of our regular school day, from 6 A.M to 7 A.M every Friday morning. I would teach him my Health content, including objectives and evaluation techniques. He would teach me how to use the many Quality Tools that would help the students master the objectives. He sacrificed his break times and came in to one of my classes every day. The success we witnessed was almost instantaneous! We even observed students who had been indifferent about school absolutely blossom and become excited about learning. It was a beautiful thing! We hung many of the artifacts each team produced in the hallways of the school for all to see.

Many teachers began asking what we were doing to produce such results. They recognized the names of many of their indifferent students on the artifacts. We held after-school workshops for any interested teachers. Eventually we offered in-service workshops to many different school districts in eastern Iowa. We were featured presenters at the Iowa School Board Conference in Des Moines; I wrote an article about our project for a Superintendents Journal.

Meanwhile, back in the classroom, we knew the students were ready to solve "real world problems" out in the community. We were able to place teams at the local newspaper, at a large paper mill, at an avionics company, and at a non-profit organization. The businesses were asked to identify a problem they were currently facing; the students used the Quality Tools to come up with solutions and then did presentations, with visuals, of a solution. The solutions were well-received and the students felt like valued adults!

Although it was very rewarding to team-teach with our new Superintendent, Dr. P, I eventually was brave enough to go solo with the Quality Tools in all my classes. All the instructional learning packets we had prepared had shifted responsibility to the learners; in essence, I had worked my way out of a job as a teacher in my own classroom and now I was a facilitator.

The "proof was in the pudding" moment happened several months later. I was one of two mentor trainers who worked with new mentor teachers and their mentees. Dr. P was present at that workshop. About 20 minutes into our workshop, the Principal came in and asked if I had a substitute in my classroom for the day. I told him that I had applied for one and had heard nothing to make me think that she was not coming. He said one of the student supervisors had stepped into my classroom and saw the "strangest thing he had ever seen". The student supervisor told the Principal that he could see an agenda board; he could see teams with instruction packets, and it appeared that they were helping each other to learn; he could see material supplies spread out on the tables. He saw no off-task behavior and no discipline issues, and he could see NO TEACHER in the classroom!

I knew a substitute would only need to facilitate, but I also knew my students would take charge of their own learning. The new mentor teachers and their mentees in the workshop were absolutely blown away! Dr. P sent a wink in my direction. We could not have created any more interest in learning if we had planned it....

The Love Ladder Climb

Self-Esteem is an individual's evaluation of their own self-worth. How they feel about themselves is directly related to a person's success in school and to the quality of their relationships.

For whatever reason, by the time they reach High-School, some students feel very poorly about themselves. They have grown up with beliefs that they are not "enough", that they don't matter in this world, that their feelings are all wrong, or that they don't even deserve to be respected. Low esteem is learned and when a student has low esteem, it affects all aspects of their life. It is for this reason that Health classes teach about self-esteem, and how to achieve and maintain a positive outlook. Units that address these issues in my class included character development, assertiveness training, and the climb up the Love Ladder. Yes, you read that correctly- the Love Ladder.

The Love Ladder had 10 steps that a person "climbs" from childhood to adulthood, beginning at the bottom with Love of Self. At that bottom rung a baby learns they must be loveable because when they cry, they are fed, burped, and cradled; if a baby is abandoned or left alone to cry, he feels differently about himself and doesn't smile as often as the child who is taken care of. The climb up the ladder has a necessary and different learning experience at each step and describes the positive outcomes of achieving success at that stage and age, or the negative affects if the step is missed or skipped on the way to the top rung. It progresses through stages such as Love of the Nurturer where the power of modeling is strong, through Love of Peers, Love of the Opposite Sex-Older, Love of the ONE (infatuation), all the way to the top rung of Unconditional Love. It was a high interest topic and because I teach through stories or analogies, it was usually fun, and sometimes embarrassing for me.

Love of the Opposite Sex-Older is the level where a person admires an adult in their life and safely practices flirtation with that adult because he or she is considered a "safe person" in their life with whom they can perfect these charms. The older person might be an aunt or uncle, or the parent of children they babysit, or a neighbor, or a teacher in their life. The description of this level points out that it is a perfectly normal and natural stage in the development of love unless the older person takes advantage of your feelings. Of course, the students in my classroom wanted to know if I had ever felt that way about any of my teachers. I told them my story: "When I was a senior in high-school I was in LOVE with my Math teacher Mr. B who, of course, had no idea as to my feelings about him. I would pretend to be 'stupid' so he would come to my desk and personally tutor me. His after shave smelled amazing. On a good day, he would move my hand off my paper so he could see my work and the skin touching was exciting. Mr. B was happily married to a beautiful wife, but that was okay because my feelings and flirting never left the classroom. Yeah, I was in LOVE with him!"

My students would be somewhat comforted because of their own experiences at this level.

And then I added to the story: "I married a Math teacher myself and I shared this story with him because he recognized the flirtations in his own classroom, especially his first year of teaching. Well, my husband and I went back to my hometown for my niece's confirmation, and low and behold, who should be sitting in one of the front pews but my high-school Math teacher, Mr. B! The one I LOVED! He looked as handsome as ever. His daughter was a member of the confirmation class, too. I pointed out my former Math teacher to my husband and told him that, now that I was a teacher myself, I should tell Mr. B how I felt. My hus-band said, 'I dare you'. Well, I saw that dare as a challenge, so when the church service was finished, I marched right up to him and said, 'Mr. B, you probably don't even remember me, but I was a student in your Col-lege-Prep Math class and now I am a teacher myself and my husband is a Math teacher like you. Well, ah, I want to tell you something, but I know I will be totally embarrassed so I will say good-bye first and then tell you what I want to say. So, 'good-bye.' At this point my voice started sounding child-like and I was rambling. I remember talking about his after shave and his hand touching my own. I remember that I told him that my husband dared me to tell him. I remember my husband starting to laugh at my side. At the end of my ramblings I remember saying 'I LOVED you' and then I turned around and started to walk off, very red-faced. My husband was laughing harder now. And then Mr. B took me by the elbow and turned me around to face him and said, and I quote, "You think I didn't know?!" Oh, my goodness, I almost had to pick my husband up from the floor because he was laughing that hard!"

My students couldn't stop laughing at my story, either. I bet they will never forget the climb up the Love Ladder!

The Thief

Too many students don't like coming to school to learn. Of those, some are also discipline problems. Vanessa fit the latter category. She was a small person, but she was powerful enough to throw chairs at people or start fights with anyone who even looked cross-eyed at her!

We teachers had been informed that Vanessa had temper tantrum issues, even as a sophomore in high school. It was decided that when she knew she was about to lose control of her temper she should go to a "safe" place to cool down. Safe places included counselor's offices, the nurse, the Principal, or any teacher who had a prep time. The strategy seemed to be paying off.

One day I was just heading to my office for my prep period when Vanessa came down the hallway with more anger than I had ever seen. I tried to calm her down and could see she needed to get away from the school for a break. Since I had lunch after my prep period, that meant that I had a little over an hour to give to Vanessa. I called the main office and told them that I was taking Vanessa out for lunch. They trusted my decision explicitly. I got my purse out of the filing cabinet and we left the school. We went to a fast food restaurant and had an enjoyable lunch and an even more enjoyable conversation. We were both back in time for our respective classes. I hugged Vanessa and told her to make smart choices the rest of the day.

It was about an hour later when a student was sent to my classroom with something in her hand. It was my wallet. She had found it in the wastebasket of the girls' bathroom, devoid of its money. I knew who had taken it; Vanessa had seen where I had put my purse after we got back to school from lunch. I called the front office and told them what had happened.

The Principal had summoned Vanessa into his office and told her that a teacher's wallet had been found in the girls' bathroom and wanted to know if she knew anything about it. Her response was "I would never steal from Mrs. Olson". Because the Principal had not mentioned the teacher's name, he knew then that she had stolen it. He escorted her to my room to make an apology. I told Vanessa that I felt violated, and that if she needed money for something all she would have had to do was to ask me for it. I would have gladly helped her out. I then hugged her and we both cried. My $20 was not on her person or in her backpack.

That night Vanessa was arrested for shoplifting at a local grocery store. She had a $20 bill in her pocket at the time.

Vanessa dropped out of school before she graduated from high school. I have often wondered what ever happened to her after that....

As for me-I started locking my purse in the filing cabinet.

Monkey-See, Monkey-Do

One stipulation of getting the Home-Economics position at the school I eventually called "home" until my retirement years was that I would establish an on-sight daycare class utilizing high-school students in the "teacher" role. There obviously was a real need for such a program in our community because I only had to advertise that first year to get participants. After the initial year, word-of-mouth filled our program, including a waiting list. The free admission was the right price, and the more than one-on-one attention the preschoolers received from the high-school students was a huge drawing card. Although another teacher took over teaching the class when I became a full-time Health teacher, the program was still going strong when I retired from teaching 27 years later. I was able to see some of my original preschoolers become "teachers" in the preschool when they became high-schoolers themselves.

The high-school students worked in teams of three to plan, execute, and evaluate teaching days. They learned the skills of motivation and discipline along with how to teach about numbers and the alphabet. They planned activities that utilized social skills, stories, music, games, seat work, and play. There were two classes back-to-back, so the preschoolers were there for three hours daily, on Monday, Wednesday, and Friday. It was rewarding for me to see high-school young adults become so animated around preschoolers. It was a win-win situation for both age groups.

There are many memorable days in the preschool experience, but two stand out the most. One memory involved a high school boy named John. He was popular among his peers, a good student and an even nicer young man. Some days John came in sporting a baseball cap while other days he did not don one. I noticed that on days that John was wearing a hat, all the preschool boys would run to their cubby and retrieve their baseball cap and wear it, just like John. On hatless days for John, their hats remained in their cubbies. I relayed this to the high-school class on a workday, to explain the power of modeling. As a class we decided John should wear his hat, then take it off, then wear it again, backwards. The power of modeling was proven as we watched the preschoolers do *exactly* what John did. It was a powerful lesson about "monkey see, monkey do".

John is now in a very powerful position to model positive behaviors as a middle-school counselor.

The other memory that stands out so clearly was the day the team who was teaching had invited a spokesperson from the Humane Society to bring a menagerie of animals to the preschool. The high- schoolers were seated in a large circle with the preschoolers in a smaller circle inside of that. The spokesperson and the animals were in the center of the inner circle. The spokesperson from the Humane Society had just relayed to the preschoolers that if they had pets at home, the care of the pets wasn't just their parent's responsibility and that they should help care for them, too. She relayed that pets are a lot of fun to have, but they can be very messy. "Little Johnny", as we called him to not be confused with "big John", piped up and said, "oh I know, we have cats at our house and they S H I T all over the place!" Fortunately, I had taught the high-schoolers about the concept of extinction, so they held their laughs at bay. They were all successful of not encouraging the behavior of swearing by laughing. All except two people-yours truly and the student next to me. Jay and I managed to exit the classroom before we belly laughed for a solid 20 minutes!

"Little Johnny" grew up to be a teacher, also. I have no idea if he has cats at his house.

Band means More than Music

All three of our children were in band from junior-high until they graduated from Linn-Mar High-School. Sara, who was four years ahead of her siblings, played the clarinet; Jenni played clarinet and was in Color Guard in the football season; Jay was a drummer-an exuberant drummer. Many memories can be had from those band days...

Our youngest two are only 11 months apart in age, but they were in the same grade-level in school. Throughout their elementary years Jay and Jenni were in the same building, but they had different teachers. The high-school was a blending of all the elementary students which meant that any given student knew about 1/3 of their classmates at the start of their fresh-man year. Our children were both in the marching band- Jenni was a flag girl and Jay played the quads-so they attended summer band camp to-gether. Because Jenni's birthday was in August and Jay's birthday was coming up in September, they were the same age during summer band camp. Jay was quite a lady charmer and the girls in the band thought he was "pretty cool" so when they learned that Jenni was his sister, the girls would ask her questions about him. They asked what grade Jay was in, and she would tell them; when they asked what grade she was in, she would tell them the same answer. "Oh, so you are twins?" they would ask. Jenni would respond "No..." The next question was to ask Jay's age and Jenni would say 14; when they asked her age, she would say 14. "Oh, so you are twins?" they would ask again. Jenni would respond "No..." And then she would walk off with her best friends, grinning. Jenni loved band camp!

Each year our city hosts a parade in honor of their heritage called the Swamp Fox Parade. It is always held at the end of September, so the beautiful weather brings everybody and his brother to the event. The parade included floats, tractors, fire trucks, business equipment, police cruisers, walking youth groups, political hopefuls, horses and marching bands from both the high-schools in our town. Our two youngest children were members of our school marching band; their crisp uniforms included fancy plumed hats and white spats covering their shoes. Our school's band was immediately behind horses who had left warm, soft clumps on the pavement as they passed by the onlookers. Jenni was a member of the Color Guard, so her vision allowed her to look down and avoid stepping into the mushy clumps. Jay was a drummer and carried a set of quads so he could only see straight ahead. Fortunately for him, we were standing close to one of those warm, soft clumps and when Jay came into earshot, my husband said very clearly, "S I D E-step!" With fancy footwork, Jay avoided a calamity. He winked at his Dad and continued marching.

One evening my husband and I were doing schoolwork in our living room. Joining us were our two youngest children and four of their friends. (Our oldest daughter Sara was away in her first year of college) Partially into the evening Jay and Jenni had to leave for about a half an hour to play in the pep band during halftime of a basketball game. The other four boys did not play in the band, so they stayed planted in front of the television. The show they were watching was an amusing sitcom so there was quite a bit of laughing and loud commentary. My husband Steve stopped what he was working on, looked around the room, and said "what's wrong with this picture?" It did seem unusual that, of the four kids watching TV, eating our snacks and drinking our pop, NONE were our own children!

One evening in their senior year of high school, Jay and Jenni asked if they could host a party for band members at our home. The whole band. All of them. We said "sure" because band members are notoriously known for being good students who are too busy to make dumb choices. We readied for the event by buying bags of chips and party snacks and cases of pop, baking cookies and brownies, and ordering dozens of pizzas. Let it be said that the Olson's let no one go away hungry.

The guests had all arrived and everything was going smoothly. We realized then that band members are also notoriously LOUD. My husband and I decided that we could trust these kids enough to remove ourselves from the noise, so we went to a movie at a local theater.

Two hours later we returned to our home. Every light in the house was ablaze, music could be heard from a block away, and there was a police car in front of our home. We pulled up next to the police car and asked if there was a problem. The policeman said there was a wild party going on, probably with underage drinking and maybe even drugs. We asked why he didn't ring the doorbell to check out the situation. He told us that unless he had permission to go in, or he heard gunshots, or he received a phone call complaint, his hands were tied. My husband told him we were the homeowners and he had our permission to enter the home. He seemed surprised.

The officer found nothing but dozens of kids having a good time. The only beverages were pop and there were no drugs stronger than aspirin. The kids even asked if he would like some pizza or a brownie!

When he left, the policeman said that in all his years of being a policeman he had never seen a party that size with nothing but good, clean fun.

Band members are notoriously known for being good students who are too busy to make dumb choices.

Our oldest child, Sara, continued playing clarinet into her college years at my alma mater. Band members in college begin their year well before all the other students can check-in so that they have ample practice sessions. Sara has a late summer birthday, so I contacted the marching band director to see if I could bring decorated cupcakes to help celebrate her 18th birthday. He assured me that they would be most welcomed. They were, and all 150 band members yelled, "We love you, Sara's Mom".

Thirty-two years later, Sara's daughter turned 18 in the summer during band camp at her Mom's alma mater. Sara and I took 300 gold frosted purple cupcakes (school colors) for the whole band and they sang "Happy Birthday" to Olivia. Every band member said thank you; we decided the myth about starving college kids really was true.

Who doesn't Love
a Gingerbread House!

One (of several) of the conditions to being offered the teaching position at my last and final school was for me to establish a student chapter of FHA (Future Homemakers of America). The student group generated many ideas for the program of studies: learning cake decorating, hosting a free safe Halloween party for young children, selling decorated Valentine cookies, caroling at local nursing homes, having guest speakers in interesting careers, having an overnight lock-in at the school, going on field trips, and adopting needy families for the holidays. It was a very ambitious agenda, but we managed to complete the list in that first year.

Our favorite project was the "Adopting Needy Families for the Holidays" project. That first year we contacted HACAP (Hawkeye Area Community Action Program) and got a list of 10 needy families in the metropolitan area. We were given permission to personally deliver the presents to their homes during the holidays. I called each of the 10 families to explain our project, got sizes of each family member, and asked if there were any special requests. The FHA members collected gently used clothing and toys, sorted the donations according to ages and sizes, and wrapped an equal number of gifts for each family member. If we were missing anything from the wish list, many FHA members bought a new item to fill the void. We advertised for food donations from staff and students at our school and asked for and received free hams and milk from a local grocery store. We packed multiple vehicles, including maintenance department trucks, and procured adult volunteer drivers, including my two other department members. I made maps of our delivery route for all the drivers because GPS was still on the drawing board somewhere, and cell phones were not an "item" yet. Our caravan took off in the snow. It was still daylight when we began our adventure, but Iowa winters get dark early, so we relied on flashlights to find house numbers. One of my department members went the wrong way on a one-way street, one driver got stuck in a snowbank, and I slipped on an icy porch and scraped my back on the edge of a step. Other than that, every student and every adopted family had the holiday spirit that evening!

The next year there was no doubt in anyone's mind that we would repeat the adoption program. We got 20 family names this time and began the collection process. We wanted to give more food boxes to each family but didn't know how to increase collections. The *Good Housekeeping* magazine held an annual Gingerbread Contest with a monetary award, and it caught my Mom's eye. She said with my cake decorating skills I should enter the contest. My entry was a large farmhouse bedecked with hundreds of pieces of candy. It was so big that it took four people to carry the board it was on! I did not win the contest. Not even honorable mention. And now I had this LARGE farmhouse on my hands. We decided to have the gingerbread house on display at a local bank and raffle it off for $1 donations. Each day after school I emptied the locked box housing the donations. The money was slowly adding up, the operative word being "slowly". After all, who had a place big enough to display a LARGE farmhouse if they won the raffle! I was in my classroom several days into the project when there was a knock on my door. A stranger was there, a kind looking older gentleman. He asked if I was the one responsible for the gingerbread farmhouse on display at the local bank. I said if he was interested in owning it, he could put his donation in the locked box at the bank. He said he wasn't interested in winning (probably because it was so LARGE!), but he wanted to help our cause. He handed an envelope to me and said there are only two stipulations: 1) I shouldn't try to learn his name, and 2) I couldn't open the envelope until he left my room. Well, I tell you, no one's thoughts were on learning about Health anymore; everyone was excited to see what was in the envelope! One student checked the hallway to see if the gentleman was gone. He was. "Open it! Open it!" was the battle cry. Inside...wait for it...wait for it, were five crisp $100 bills! That bought volumes of food for the families that year. It also meant more vehicles and more drivers. We almost needed a parade permit! The LARGE gingerbread farmhouse was won by a church who said they were going to let their young parishioners get a sugar high after the holiday pageant.

The next year, our project was so well-known that more and more donations of clothing and toys came in, so by that third year we decided to adopt 25 families. It was quite an ambitious undertaking to coordinate. We were able to take over an empty classroom for sorting and wrapping the gifts. Food donations had also increased, but we reminisced about the kind "Santa Claus" that had come the year before. Dare we hope he would appear at my door again? Our wish came true. He still had the same two stipulations, and inside the envelope was a note stating that Mr. and Mrs. Claus were retiring to Arizona and wouldn't be in our area to help the following year, but he knew we would be blessed somehow. This year he did not give us five crisp $100 bills. He gave us ten crisp $100 bills! Ten...! We decided to use some of the money to buy one new outfit and one new toy for each of the family members. I made the arrangements for an after-school shopping trip at a local K-Mart and the store decided to give us a 10% discount on all the items we purchased. KCRG, the local news station got wind of our planned activity and cameras rolled as we filled that K-Mart with holiday cheer.

I was the keeper of the money, so I was standing near the checkout counter and keeping track of purchases (I had designated the amount of money each family could spend). I overhead one young mother tell several other of our adoptees that she was so grateful to our group because she was enrolled in a community college to become a nurse, and she had just had to pay $100 for textbooks, which meant her child would receive very meager gifts under their tree. After all the shopping was done and the beaming adopted families had left the store, the clerk figured out my bill. I had been keeping close track of the purchases but didn't realize that some of the chosen toys were on sale, so I ended up $99 long! My daughter, Jenni, was riding with me and I shared what I had overheard. She said "Mom, I have a dollar on me. That would make the amount exactly $100." We stopped at our local bank to have all the bills exchanged for one $100 bill and drove to the apartment of the young aspiring nurse. She looked confused about why we were at her door. I told her what I had overheard, and that we wanted to help her with her textbook bill. Jenni handed her the $100 bill and her legs buckled under her and she dropped to the floor, weeping. Her young son was confused about why she was crying, and she explained to him that these were happy tears. She told us that someday she wanted to help others out, just like we had helped her. Several years later she did send a note to our school saying that she had gotten her nursing degree and was dating a young doctor. That gave me happy tears.

The next year, Santa Claus was in Arizona, so I decided to make small, centerpiece size gingerbread houses to raffle off at all the musical concerts and home basketball games. We also placed three houses at the local bank. We took in ample money to feed our 25 families.

It's okay that I didn't win the gingerbread house contest sponsored by *Good Housekeeping* magazine. They contacted me about our project! You can read our story on page 128 of the December,1988 edition. The article is called "Isn't This What Christmas Is All About?" One picture on that page is of the LARGE farmhouse.

The FHA chapter members adopted families in all 27 years of my teaching experience at that school.

Jeff turns 18

Child Development was a class designed to have up to 20 preschoolers interact with 20-24 high-school students three days a week; on the other two days of the week the high schoolers, mostly juniors and seniors, learned concepts that could be utilized in their future as parents or teachers or daycare workers. The high school students were dubbed as "big people" while the preschoolers we referred to as "little people". The big people taught in pairs; each pair was in charge for two or three days in the semester. When they weren't the designated teacher, the high school students assisted the head teachers so that every little person had at least one big person helper. It was enjoyable watching the interaction between the big people and the little people.

Jeff was the only male enrolled in one section of Child Development that semester. He had a mischievous smile and a personality to match. The little people loved working and playing with him. The big people also enjoyed working with him. He didn't mind being the only male role model in that class!

Jeff was a hard worker both in the classroom and outside the classroom. His family had enough for their needs but not always enough for their wants. Jeff had a goal to better himself in life. I had no doubt he would achieve his goals! When I taught the concept of intellectual growth, a person's IQ was of high interest to the students. The question came up about how you could know what your IQ was. I told the students that the information could be accessed by their parents, or themselves when they became of age, in the Guidance Department.

Jeff's 18th birthday was just around the corner. Since it was his habit to always come flying into the classroom just as the final bell rang, it gave the rest of the class and me a few minutes each day before his arrival to plan a surprise birthday party for him. I said I would furnish a decorated cake. One girl said she would bring ice cream, another would bring punch, another volunteered to bring napkins, and another said she could bring cups and small plates.

The big day arrived. I had decorated the cake with a die-cast car on the top because Jeff had mentioned once that he didn't have his own car. There was vanilla ice cream and lemonade and blue paper products. One girl had come to class extra early to hang streamers and balloons that she had brought to add to the festivities. Everyone was excited to see the look of surprise on Jeff's face.

The last bell rang. Jeff did not come running in to the room at the last minute. We were disappointed. We decided that he must have taken the day off because it was his birthday. Would we have to celebrate without him? Just then the door flew open and the grinning birthday boy came running in, apologizing for being late. We told him we were afraid that he wasn't going to show up and he said, "Now that I am 18, I could go to the counseling office and find out what my IQ is!" We all laughed and asked if he was smart; he said "of course".

Years later, the adult Jeff told me that he still has the die-cast car. He is a Nuclear Manager today. I knew he would reach his goals!

To Michael, with Love

Since his growth spurt in 7th-grade, Michael had grown no further. As a senior in high-school, the tall, lanky boy was teased by his friends about wearing the same two shirts he had worn since junior-high. He said, "hey, they still fit, so why not?" He alternated wearing his two shirts every other day. The teasing did not affect Michael; he took it in stride. I overheard the teasing as Michael and his peers were entering my classroom one day.

I asked Michael's counselors about his homelife and learned that he and his sisters were being raised by a single parent. The family was receiving food stamps but there was still extra month at the end of his Mom's paycheck. They could not afford new clothes like the other students had come to expect.

I wanted to help Michael if I could but did not want him to feel like a charity case. In my mind I was thinking that a new shirt for his graduation ceremony would be a nice gesture. I shared my thoughts with my family. They liked the idea but had the same hesitancy that I had; we did not want to have Michael feel uncomfortable about accepting help.

Helping Michael was on my mind for days. My daughter Sara and I were shopping at a local mall when we found a "perfect" shirt for her. I spotted a Hawaiian-print shirt that I thought was pretty and decided to try it on myself since Sara was already in a dressing room. As I was looking at the label to check the care instructions, I looked at the brand. It was "To Michael, with Love"! I excitedly yelled out the information to Sara and said that I felt like I had just received confirmation that helping Michael was the "right thing" to do!

Together my family and I hatched a plan to help Michael. It did involve stretching the truth a bit. The next day in class I took Michael off to the side during class work time and told him that each year my family liked to help out one senior by buying them new clothes for graduation, and this year (here's the truth stretching) his name was pulled out of the hat as being the winner! He said "Really? Cool!" We made plans to go shopping the next evening.

Sara and I picked Michael up at his home and headed for the mall. After browsing the stores for what I thought was appropriate attire, we came upon a Madras plaid shirt that caught Michael's eye. My idea of what was conservatively appropriate was not his idea of what he would like to wear for graduation. I did not argue the point at all because he was the one that was going to wear the shirt, not me. We purchased it and headed for the car. Michael said he liked the shirt but what he had always wanted to own was a Chicago Cubs shirt, but he knew that would not be "cool" for the graduation ceremony. I said that we should head back into the mall and get one. He argued that I had already bought the Madras plaid shirt and that his Mom would be disappointed if he showed up in a sport-type shirt. After I convinced him that I wanted to buy both for him we found the Cubs shirt and gingerly went back to the car.

Michael was in the back seat. I could see in the rear-view mirror that he was taking the tags off the Cubs shirt with his teeth! He slipped the new shirt on and had the biggest grin on his face. Sara and I felt humbled. I asked if Michael had supper plans and he said, "just our usual mac and cheese". I told him that we had no plans and wondered if he would like to go to a fast food drive-through with us. He hesitated and I knew it was because he had no money on him. When I said it would be my treat he said, "are you sure? You already bought these shirts for me." I insisted. He enjoyed 2 cheeseburgers, super-sized fries, and a large drink. Sara and I enjoyed seeing him wolf it down!

Our shopping excursion occurred two-weeks before graduation. The day after our shopping adventure Michael came to school sporting his new Cubs shirt. His friends gave him compliments and he beamed. The next day he donned the Madras plaid shirt and again, the classmates complimented him. The next day it was the Cubs shirt, the day after that was the Madras, and then he repeated that pattern for the rest of the two weeks.

On graduation day, Michael looked so handsome and proud in his new Madras plaid shirt. His grin was big and genuine as he hugged me and humbly said "Thanks, Mrs. Olson. You're the best...."

A Real Cinderella Story

Sometimes High-School kids can be cruel. Sometimes their idea of "fun" is at the expense of others. Sometimes the victim is very unsuspecting. Such is the case with Kristine.

Kristine was a freshman that year. She lived with her sister and her mom in a small rented home. Her mom, mainly out of necessity, sewed all her daughters' clothes. Kristine looked homespun among her peers. No one could have predicted that she would become a victim. But she did.

It was Fall football season, which meant it was Homecoming time. One girl and one boy, elected by their own classmates, would represent the 9th-through-11th-grade class; the seniors were represented by five couples, elected by the whole student body. Because it is possible that no one could be a winner if everyone voted for themselves, it only takes a handful of votes to have a majority to elect a candidate at the 9-11th-grade level. All the candidates were to be revealed during a pep rally one week before Homecoming.

The entire student body had assembled on the bleachers of the gym. As a faculty member, I had to take a seat amongst students rather than with teachers. Crowd control, they called it. A group of freshmen boys surrounded my seat. The emcee had just stepped up to the podium to announce the 9th-grade candidates. I could hear a handful of boys who were snicker-whispering behind me. When Kristine's name was announced, there was total silence. Everyone expected a cheerleader or a dance squad member to be the candidate, after all, their names were more popular. No one came forward. The emcee called Kristine's name a second time. Across the gym floor, where the band members were seated, I could see movement. Someone had tapped the arm of the trumpet player, the new 9th-grade candidate, who obviously thought there must be some mistake. The emcee called her name a third time, and slowly and very humbly, Kristine came forward. The handful of boys behind me high-fived each other. I knew right away what had happened with the voting.

That Friday night a group of cheerleaders and dance squad members had a sleepover at one of their homes. By this time the handful of boys had "bragged" about how they kept any of them from becoming the homecoming candidate. The girls were furious at the boys, wistful because the winner was none of them, and embarrassed for Kristine. The mother in that home overheard the conversation. Together, they all hatched a plan. That's when my name crossed their thoughts.

Monday morning at school I was contacted about the hatched plan. It had been decided that Kristine's Mom could probably not afford formalwear for the coronation that next Thursday. The cheerleader and dance squad Mom's had collected $200 for an outfit for her and wanted me to take her shopping. My first thought was "why me?" My second thought was "why not me?"

I called Kristine that night to congratulate her and told her that a group of adults who really enjoyed helping students out, had chosen the female freshman candidate to be the recipient of their generosity this year. I was not prepared for her response. She said, "thank you, but my

Mom and I picked out fabric and she has already started making my dress." I'm not sure where my quick thinking came from when I suggested we buy new shoes and jewelry and undergarments to go with the new dress. I was very relieved when she quickly responded, "okay".

The next evening, I picked up Kristine and her Mom and I reimbursed them for the cost of the fabric for the dress and then headed for the mall. We found shoes and undergarments and jewelry, and I still had money left over. I asked the Mom if she would like a new outfit to wear at the half-time introduction of the candidates and their parents. She was in disbelief and said she hadn't had anything new for herself in years. The leftover money bought her a new pantsuit and a pair of shoes. I don't ever remember seeing such gratitude prior to that night!

Good things happen to those who deserve it. A local optometrist volunteered giving Kristine eye contacts so she wouldn't need to wear her bottle-thick glasses anymore; a beautician volunteered to style Kristine's hair into a more modern cut; a nail salon donated a manicure and a pedicure; a make-up artist gave Kristine a facial and make-up.

The night of the coronation, everyone was assembled in the gym. I purposely chose my seat near the boys who felt smug about stacking the voting box. I wanted to see their faces. The freshman candidates were announced first. I could hear the handful of 9th-grade boys snicker-whispering behind me. Then Kristine and the male candidate came through the door. Kristine looked amazing! She was the vision of royalty. Her new looks gave her confidence for the first time in forever. I didn't have to see the faces of those boys because I could hear their reaction. They had inadvertently elected the most beautiful, most humble, and most deserving girl in their class to represent the 9th-grade. The last laugh was on them.

I would like to say that this experience changed Kristine's outlook on life, and it absolutely did. She walked with more confidence in the hallways. Her peers included her in conversations afterwards. And yet, she remained humble throughout her high school years.

Sometimes high-school kids can be cruel. Sometimes their idea of "fun" is at the expense of others. Sometimes the victim is very unsuspecting. Sometimes lemons can be made into lemonade. Such was the case with Kristine.

Choose a Sense of Humor

You've likely been told that it takes less muscles to smile than it does to frown; frowning requires working 43 muscles and smiling requires 17. One of the best ways to bring a smile to a student's face is by having the teacher use humor in the classroom.

Humor always works well for me. If I trip, I say "I meant to do that". If you trip, I say, "enjoy your trip; see you in the Fall". Humor can help everyone "save face". Humor also lowers levels of concern, things that can cause fear and anxiety that eventually undermine concentration and learning. As a full-time teacher I used humorous examples and analogies, I searched the comic strips for content that applied to my curriculum, I posted inspirational posters in the classroom, I used cartoon stickers when grading papers, and I read amusing stories to drive home a point. And if a student said or did something that brought positive laughter, I laughed with him not at him. I have even belly-laughed more times than I can count; that causes everyone to have a good laugh. Laughter and humor strengthen relationships. In my classroom, laughter and humor was the cement that held the group together.

Now that I am in the substitute teaching years of my career, I need to use humor to establish a good rapport, as well. Substitutes are confined to the curriculum plans provided to us, so don't have the privilege of planning specific examples or analogies, so I introduce a humorous story at the start of each class. Telling the story focuses attention to the front of the room, quiets the students down so they can hear, and establishes a bit of levity. I have a binder full of stories I have heard from others or read in a magazine or pulled off the internet. The stories in the binder are organized by content and age so I can quickly find what I need. I try to personalize the stories by referencing local places or streets in our community or activities near and dear to their age group to bring more interest to them.

Sometimes a personalized story brings an unexpected response, as in this story. "Four little old gray-haired ladies from Anamosa decided to drive to Central City for lunch. They had just turned the corner by Walmart out here, when a state trooper pulled them over. He asked if they knew why he pulled them over. The driver said that she didn't know why because she was obeying all the rules of the road. He explained that typically he pulls over speeders, but in this case, she was driving too slowly. She begged to differ with him, saying she was going the speed limit that was posted. He asked what she meant, so she pointed to the sign. It said 13. The policeman rubbed his forehead and told the little old lady that 13 wasn't the speed limit, it was the highway number, Highway 13. Just then he got a good look at all the riders in her car and realized they were all disheveled and looked petrified. He knew right away what had happened. They had just been on Highway 151!" The students like this story and believe it is real because of the highway numbers. But, now and then, I get the unexpected question, "Were you the driver, Mrs. Olson?" Then we start the class with added humor.

Having a sense of humor is part of the art of getting along with people. Teachers need to remember to use it.

Connected at the Hip

Teachers like to have fun on Spring Break, just as much as students. Twenty-three staff members from our school district decided to spend our vacation in Las Vegas. I had never been there before, so I was excited about the trip. My husband Steve had no desire to go, so he stayed home and had peace and quiet.

One of our granddaughters, Brittan, and I were "attached at the hip". She felt happy and safe in my care, and I couldn't spend enough time with her. She was about three at the time of the Vegas trip and didn't understand that people can leave on an airplane and come back on an airplane. She thought an airplane took you away for forever. Her Mom, our daughter Jenni, tried to allay her fears; she even gave Brittan a silver dollar to give me for luck, hoping she would understand that my absence wasn't going to be permanent. She arranged to have Brittan be at the airport when I returned, but even that didn't turn off the waterworks-hers and mine- as the plane departed.

The trip was every bit as exciting as I had hoped. Real often, anticipation is greater than reality, but Vegas did not disappoint. We took tours, went to shows, watched the street attractions, witnessed beggars, and hit the slots. One of our cab drivers was correct, though, when he told us that the only way to leave Vegas with $1000 was to begin with $2000. We had fun on Spring Break! And what happens in Vegas, stays in Vegas, or so the saying goes.

My husband Steve, daughter Jenni, and granddaughter Brittan were going to pick me up upon our arrival back home. It was a rainy evening. The passengers from the plane entered the terminal on the upper level, and visitors had to remain on the lower level. An escalator connected the two floors; guards were seated at the bottom of the escalators. I was half-way down the escalator when Brittan spotted me. She jumped off Jenni's lap and, like a bullet, ran past the guards and up the moving escalator to leap into my arms. Everyone was laughing. The guards said they couldn't have stopped her if they had wanted to! As we left the terminal for the car, the rain mingled with the waterworks, our tears of joy. Everyone else had to carry my belongings because my arms were full of love; there was no way Brittan was going to let go of her gramma. After all, we are connected at the hip.

Homecoming is in the Air

omecoming is synonymous with leaves changing colors, bon fires, kings and queens, football games, decorated class-rooms and hallways, and parades. Our school celebrated for a full week, and suggestions for attire were determined by the Student Council: Monday was pajama day, Tuesday was twin day, Wednesday was cartoon character day, Thursday was color day, and Friday was school spirit day. Most of the students and a large percent of the faculty had fun choosing their clothing in that special week.

The parade on the Thursday night before the Friday night football game spewed the enthusiasm into the community as floats throwing candy, sport teams throwing candy, bands, youth groups throwing candy, and the kings and queens in Corvettes took to the streets of the town. At the head of the parade was the "Grand Marshall", typically a city official or dignitary.

In this particular year, for who knows what reason, the student body decided the role should honor a staff member. I became the first teacher-turned-Grand Marshall. It was quite an honor until I realized it meant that I had to sit on top of the back seat of the moving Corvette convert-ible and perform the "royal wave", the wave that involves a vertical hand with a slight twist from the wrist. My farm-girl upbringing was devoid of learning the "royal wave". I had even been the Homecoming queen in my own High-School, but I had just used the "farm wave", the one where you raise one or two fingers off the steering wheel as a friendly greeting to fellow farmers.

The parade was lining up for take-off when the Corvette hosting the two freshman representatives decided to rebel. It was incapable of going anywhere! Plan B had to be put into action; those two students would ride in the lead car with the Grand Marshall. The male candidate sat down in the front seat by the driver, and the female candidate and I sat on top of the back seat, performing the "royal wave". I was relieved to have company as we made our way through the parade route.

I have never ridden in a Corvette convertible or performed the "royal wave" since then, and I am just fine with that!

Kids like and need Rules— yes, they do

An age-old dilemma for parents is: should we discipline, or should we punish, or are they even the same thing? Our own upbringing often causes us to choose one over the other because "it was good enough for me and I turned out just fine".

Teachers face the same dilemma in their classes, but with 25 individuals instead of a handful of them. Because of their decision, they will have either "harmony in the feedlot" or total chaos. The latter has driven many good teachers out of the classroom and into another profession altogether.

The class rapport must be established from day ONE. Through my experience in three different school districts, I have seen a lot of teachers create a positive learning environment right from the start. I have also seen teachers that did not establish rules and discipline right from the start, and they never did regain decorum. For a teacher there is a huge difference between being liked and respected by students or being in control and disliked. The difference is finding the fine line between discipline, which is proactive, and punishment, which is reactive.

How a teacher has established guidelines in a classroom also affects how the students behave when they have a substitute in the classroom. In my almost 20 total years of substitute teaching, I have learned which teachers I can enjoy subbing for, and to whom I give a "pass". A substitute can only maintain discipline as well as, or worse, than the regular teacher because the students have been conditioned to behave in a certain way in that classroom. The exception to this rule is if the timeframe for subbing is long-term, and then you have time to re-train the expectations in that classroom. Some subs only like one-day assignments; I prefer multiple day assignments because I see the situation as a challenge if the students are used to being undisciplined. I know when I have succeeded when, on the last day, the students ask if I can be their regular teacher. Kids really do like and need rules and guidance!

Even on one-day subbing assignments, I need to maintain discipline. If the class time has started and students are still socializing, I say "Excuse me. I think I'm talking, but I'm not sure because I can't hear me". Or, I will stand at the front and say, "I'll wait..." and typically some student who is there to learn will tell the social butterflies to "knock it off"; I will thank him and we will commence with the agenda. I have never yelled at kids to be quiet, and I hope I never will. Ironically, I have had students thank me for controlling the class so they can learn!

Some retirees never want to sub because they don't have their own class, some just never want to teach again, some think kids have changed to the worse, and some use the twilight years to do other adventures. For this reason, substitutes are in high demand but in low supply. Thus, a huge advantage a substitute has is that they can have the attitude of "the school needs me more than I need them". We can be a bit daring or bold with our discipling techniques and think, "what are they going to do-fire me? I don't care!"

I once had a 6th-grade boy who was walking on top of the desks to cross the room; he was not listening to instruction and, even worse, was preventing others from hearing the instructions. Very calmly, I said "get out." He asked if I was talking to him. I said, "get out." He asked where he was supposed to go. I said "I really don't care. Just get out!" He did and everyone else was on task for the rest of the period. After class, I found him sitting on the floor outside of the room. He apologized! The next opportunity I had to sub with him in a different classroom, he told the class that they better behave for me because there are consequences to not behaving.

Another time I was subbing for a resource teacher, so my assignment was to attend classes with three-to-five resource students in a regular classroom of 25 or more students and assist as needed. One high-school resource student was wearing a head set and listening to his music rather than paying attention to the teacher. I said he needed to take the head set off. He was defiant and said he wanted to listen to his (loud) music. I said that the teacher was going over the math homework from the day before; he said that he hadn't done the work, so he didn't need to listen. I said that he could learn from listening so he would know how to do it for the next quiz. When the young girl behind him said, "at least turn your music down so I can hear", he responded that he liked it loud. I pulled the headset off his head and threw them into the closest corner of the room. He said, "Hey, you can't do that!" I responded, "Hey, I just did!" I did not get fired; the school needed me more than I needed them. Surprisingly, I saw that young man and his Mom at the local grocery store a while later, and he introduced me as "the best sub at our school"! Kids really do like and need rules and guidance!

The Double Fight

Adoppelganger is a non-biologically related look-alike or double that, supposedly, all humans have somewhere in the world. I am still looking for mine, although through the years I have been told that I remind someone of someone else.

Two boys at our school were true doppelgangers. They were not related at all, and yet they were the same height and weight, had the same hair and eye color, and their face shapes were identical. It was nearly impossible to tell them apart until you saw them in their interactions with peers. One was a gentleman with a fun sense of humor; the other was a bully whose laughs came at the expense of others. The former and I were "friends".

One day during passing time a fight broke out in the hallway outside of my classroom. Another female teacher and I were first responders before any administrator showed up. I recognized my "friend" and was amazed that he would be involved in an altercation, so I bear-hugged him from behind to pull him away from the other angry student. The other teacher did the same with the other angry student. Neither of the fighters liked being wrangled in so both were trying to break away from our bear-hugs. The student audience was orally trying to promote a continued fight because it was a good excuse for being late to their next class.

The boys were strong, and it took all our strength as we two female teachers waited for administrative back-up. We could have been accidentally hit and hurt, but I was amazingly at peace because I knew my "friend" would not hurt me. I looked around the sea of faces trying to spot any other staff member, and suddenly, I spotted my "friend" in the audience. That meant I was bear-hugging his doppelganger! I hoped my health insurance was adequate.

When the administration arrived and everything was said and done, my "friend" came into my classroom and I told him I thought it was he that I was protecting. He said, "I was watching close, Mrs. Olson, and I wouldn't let him hurt you. It didn't look like you needed any help, though." Then we high-fived.

The Importance of Katrina

My sister Millie, also a former teacher, told me once that there are two people in a school with whom you should establish a good relationship from day one, and that was the janitor and the secretary. They are like the worker bees and are often overlooked by others. Too often they are treated as secondary workers; actually, they are a teacher's biggest supporter if they are treated with respect and as an equal. Millie could not have been more correct!

Katrina was one of the hardest workers with whom I had the pleasure to work. She was the janitress in charge of the kitchen and lunchroom area, the locker rooms, the bathrooms adjacent to those areas, three Foreign Language classrooms, and the Home-Economics area where I worked. She worked with efficiency and without complaining about the messy areas to which she was assigned. If people tried to give her sympathy, she always said, "they're just kids. I don't mind the messes".

Some kids weren't lucky enough to be born into money, so didn't always have the essentials to stay warm in the Iowa winters. Katrina would use her own money to buy those kids socks or gloves. A few times she purchased bigger coats for students who had outgrown theirs several years prior.

Kids who had to wait for rides after school hung out in the lunch-room. Typically, these were students who couldn't afford their own trans-portation, and whose parents had two jobs to support their family, so their schedules meant a delay in picking up their kids right after school. Katrina had this 6th-sense about her and could figure out which kids had no extra money to buy a snack or a pop while they waited, so she would target a specific kid and ask if they could help her take trash to a dumpster, and in exchange she would buy them a treat out of her own pocket. She said then they "didn't have to have empty tummies".

Katrina was "classy". Even though her attire was jeans and a sweat-shirt, she always wore make-up like she was going to a gala affair. Her hair was always neat and trimmed. She was pencil thin and could squat with bended knees to take a break. She was in the November years of her life but had the agility of a high-school age girl. She was lavish with compliments about attire and high-heeled shoes, as though that was very important to her.

I enjoyed visiting with Katrina after school. She could talk as she worked and enjoyed the company. Sometimes I would pull the plug on her vacuum if she hadn't seen me come into the lunchroom area. She would look around to see what had happened to her machine and then spot me and she knew. With her hands on her thin hips she would say, "Madelyn!!" I missed her a lot when she retired.

I saw Katrina several years after she had hung up her brooms, and she said that she missed the kids and the staff, and that her health was going downhill due to her smoking habit. She said she could no longer squat and bend at the knees, that you really do "lose it if you don't use it". She now looked the part of someone in the November years of their life.

The last time I saw Katrina was at her funeral visitation. Her family was happy I had come. The volume of grievers was small and then I understood why she enjoyed having company while she worked. There was a display of pictures of her life. I learned that in her youth, she had been a glamorous model for a well-known cigarette company. She had been a beauty! Now, I understood her interest in clothes and shoes.

Katrina may have been the most important person in our school. I wish I had taken the time to get to know her better.

The Odor of Things

Puberty: the time when a person's body changes from a child to an adult, typically in middle-school and high-school. Often called the hormones-on-tennis-shoes stage.

Some students traverse the road to puberty with very few adjustments and end up at the finish line grasping a blue ribbon. Others have a few obstacles along the way and end up with a red ribbon. The white ribbon winners may have suffered from acne, halitosis, slouched shoulders, or body odor.

My first personal experience with the dreaded body odor occurred at about the age of 12. My Dad was a farmer and a mechanic. He had a workshop on our farmstead and neighbors brought their trucks and tractors and farm equipment for repair. He had the only welder and lathe for miles around, so he was always busy. His workshop suffered the consequences of the business. He would have my twin sisters, Nancy or Nadine, or me clean his shop on a regular basis, and he would always slip us some spending money as a thank-you. The cleaning involved straightening the dozens of tools, brushing the metallic residue from the lathe, dusting drill shavings off the workbench, and sweeping everything else off the floor. It was an arduous task but getting spending money was a motivator.

I was cleaning the shop when my Dad said, "Boots, you have B.O."
My Dad had never said anything negative to me in my life, so I determined that it must be a compliment. I asked him what that was, and he told me to go ask Mom. When she explained that B.O. meant "body odor", I was embarrassed! I didn't want to face Dad ever again, but Mom assured me that Dad would probably never bring it up again, especially if I made sure I was bathed and wore deodorant daily. I learned my lesson that day! He probably saved me from having a "white ribbon" in high school!

A definite white ribbon winner at my last school was a young man that had BO so bad that he was ripe! Christopher was a people-pleaser, especially with his teachers. He got to school early every day, probably when his peers were still at home showering. The later in the day, and the later in the week was almost unbearable for anyone in his vicinity. I had talked to the school nurse and his assigned counselor, and they gave him some soap and toiletries; their mission lasted only a few days. It didn't help that Christopher left his coat on all the time; he or it had no time to air out. Christopher was oblivious to his own aroma. I purposely did not address the issue in class because I did not want to ruin the rapport we had established. But the day of reckoning came. School was let out early due to an ice storm and Christopher usually walked the mile and a half to school from his mobile home residence, so I offered him a ride home. He graciously helped scrape the thick layer of ice off my windshield while the car was warming up. When we finally got in the car, we were glad the car was toasty warm. The heater circulated the air and it also circulated his unpleasant odor. I had to open my window a crack just to breathe. Rapport at risk or not, I had to address the stench. It came out a bit harsh, however, when I just blurted out, "Kid, you stink!" We had a discussion all the way to the trailer court where he lived, including my own experience with BO when I was 12. The bluntness paid off. The next day he came to school bathed. I asked if he wanted to leave his coat-his offensive, smelly coat- in my classroom since I was giving him a ride home again due to the still icy streets. Unbeknownst to him, I washed that coat in the washer and dryer in the Home-Economics room during the day; I ended up washing it twice before it was finally clean and fresh-smelling.

Christopher was no longer associated with a "white ribbon."

The Power of Modeling

I believe that 95% of who a student is, is learned at home. This belief is often proven when a teacher can predict what any given student's parents are like before they even meet them. "The acorn doesn't fall very far from the tree" comes to mind.

My husband and I were parents as well as teachers. One of the values we tried to instill into our children was honesty and integrity. These values are two that can't just be taught by telling them; these must also be taught through modeling. We were provided the perfect opportunity to model because of my cake decorating hobby.

The local grocery store had my favorite brand of cake mixes on sale. I sent my husband to the store to buy our other groceries and a case of the mixes. When he came home, I questioned why the bill was so low. Steve said he thought it seemed low, too, but it was the new manager who had rung up his order, so he didn't question it at the time. We finally discovered why it was so low; the manager had just charged for a single cake mix at the sale price, not the price for a case. Our three children- Sara, Jay, and Jenni- were gathered around us and asked what we were going to do about it. I used the devil-and-angel on your shoulder to model my decision: "Well, I could make more money on cakes I create, but I might feel guilty and the cakes might flop. Besides, the manager was the one who rang it up so it's okay; but it's dishonest because it's like stealing. But we can buy other things with the extra money, but I would feel like I was cheating if I used it." I almost had whiplash from turning my head side-to-side as I pretended to have the devil and the angel argue the point. Then the kids said "What are you going to do, Mommy? What are you going to do?" I told them there was only one right thing to do, and that was to return to the store with the difference that we owed them. Honesty was modeled.

Fast forward 10 years. Our son Jay was a junior in high-school and he and his girlfriend, Brenda (who now is his wife) went to the Mall to buy Christmas gifts. When Jay stepped out of his truck he nearly slipped on a large red envelope. Upon investigation, he found a card that said "Love, gramma" and $400. There was no name on the envelope and no way to find the owner. He later told me the devil-and-angel argument went through his head: nobody would know he had found it, it could buy a lot of gifts, it wasn't like he stole it because it was on the ground, BUT some other kid was missing money from his gramma and he probably didn't throw it on the ground, he probably lost it, and I would feel terrible if I was him. He took the money in to the Lost-and-Found Department. They said they would keep it and hope the rightful owner would come to claim it. Now, Steve and I "didn't raise no dummies". Jay was smart enough to say that he would hang unto it and if someone came forward, they could contact him. He gave the Lost-and-Found Department his phone number. He waited. And waited. And waited. Finally, four days after he stepped on that big red envelope, he received the call. When the gentleman could identify the contents of the red envelope, Jay knew he was the rightful owner. He told Jay that his son had saved lawn-mowing money, dog-walking money, birthday money and Christmas money and was ready to make a large purchase in the electronics store when he lost the money. The man had told his son that he was sure that the money was lost for good. They arranged to meet at a local store and, unbeknownst to Jay, the man had arranged for KCRG, a local TV station to also be at the meeting place. That night Jay was featured on the news and called a Good Samaritan. He was awarded $50 for his honesty.

Fast forward 10 more years. In a unit on Values, I shared the story of the big red envelope, using no names. A student at the back of the classroom jumped up and loudly said, "No way! I was that kid who lost the money!"

The power of modeling is potent.

Turkey Bingo

My best friend Janet, who also happened to be my in-a-pinch babysitter for my early subbing years, became a first-time mother within a week of me becoming one. The births created a bond between us that would ultimately cross over many decades.

We liked to take our new babies on walks and when we did, it was customary to carry change should we need to call our husbands from a pay phone. It was an unusually warm October that year, so we decided to take our babies out for a stroll while our husbands multi-tasked watching football on TV and playing cards.

Our children were only three months old so they could sit side-by-side in the same stroller with space to spare. Janet and I took turns pushing the stroller up and down the inclines of the sidewalks. By the time we got to the main street of town, the heat had gotten to us. We realized there was a Bingo game going on in the Community Center, so we decided to get out of the heat and sit down for a spell. Once we sat down, we decided it might be fun to play a game, so we used our emergency dimes to buy a card. We placed the kernels of corn markers on the numbers that were called- B 2, I 18, O 72... When we had filled up a row before anyone else, we yelled "BINGO"! We were giddy with excitement and couldn't believe how lucky we were until we discovered our prize was an 18-pound turkey! Eighteen pounds. That was more than the combined weight of our babies. We had no emergency phone money so we couldn't call our husbands to come pick us up. We did the only option available to us: we put the turkey in the stroller, each carried a baby in one arm and used our other arms to guide the stroller all the way home. It was still quite warm. The sidewalks had not flattened out while we played Bingo, and our babies were putting on weight as we walked.

When we finally got home and we told our husbands what had happened, they laughed and laughed. Then my husband said, "only you two could go on a stroll with two babies and come home with a full-grown turkey"!

Variety is the Spice of Life

E very teacher is unique. Every teacher has quirks and practices and styles that, if combined, would make up a beautiful patchwork quilt.

Alvin and Vicki taught in the same district; he taught in the high-school and she was a kindergarten teacher. They had been married for many years but were still on their honeymoon. Every day Vicki would pack Alvin's lunch and always included a love note. Sometimes the note was between the two pieces of bread in his sandwich, sometimes it was in the cup of his thermos bottle, sometimes it was wrapped inside a stick of gum. Those of us who shared his lunch time hovered over his lunch until the note was found. Then we would all smile and enjoy our lunch.

Phil taught Biology. He had designed a poster for his door with a caricature of a military leader whose name was "General Biology". In the classroom he was famous for comebacks and lines like "You put the wrong em-pha-sis on the right syll-a-bal". He was probably one of the pun-iest people with whom I ever had the pleasure to teach.

David had a poster in his Math class that had a picture of an octagon, a hexagon, a pentagon, and Oregon.

The shop teacher had a poster that said, "Your parents called and said they want you to bring all your fingers home."

Mary had inherited a great deal of money when her parents died. We had all gotten our monthly paycheck and were putting them in our purses or wallets when she pulled four months-worth of paychecks out of her wallet and said, "Maybe I should put these in the bank one of these days". The rest of us had extra month at the end of our money.

Cheryl taught Psychology. She wore a slip under her dresses that had "Freudian" written all over it.

Vicki always talked very softly in her kindergarten classroom. Her kids never yelled or got loud because they wanted to hear her.

Robby was such an animated vocal music director that during concerts, all eyes were on him and his exaggerated movements rather than the singers. He had rhythm!

My first Principal sometimes spoke before he thought. He was behind me in the lunch line when I politely declined a serving of sauerkraut (I call it sewer-kraut). He said, "Sauerkraut is good for you. It puts hair on your chest". Without missing a beat, I said, "But, sir. Then my undergarments wouldn't fit!"

The Foods teacher always knew the males in her class would not be able to think clean thoughts during the protein unit: the chicken breasts and legs, the turkey thighs, the pork loin, chickens laying eggs. She much preferred teaching about fruits and vegetables!

A Spanish teacher had pairs of shoes that were all the exact same style, but each pair was a different color. She could match the color of every outfit she had. The only problem was that sometimes she arrived at school wearing two different colors of shoes.

Variety is the spice of life!

A Tribute to Tabatha

I t's not easy being in High-School. There's so much drama and so much competition. Students who get involved in music or acting classes or sports or youth groups tend to weather the storm easier than students who, for whatever reason, choose to not get involved in extracurricular activities.

Tabatha belonged to the latter category, mainly for economic reasons. She often told me that she was a "nobody" and that she couldn't keep up with the standards at our high-school. She said she would never be able to dress for success. Try as I might, I could not convince her of her worth. Ironically, Tabatha was one of the prettiest girls on campus. With her long dark hair and bright brown eyes and flawless complexion, she was stunning. All of that was hidden from others because of the way she chose to be invisible. I felt bad that she graduated without knowing how beautiful she was on the inside and on the outside.

Tabatha did not have funds to attend college, so she joined the army and after basic training was deployed to Germany. She was home on leave a year later and came to the school to visit with some of her teachers, me included. She was dressed in full military uniform; her hair was shorter and styled, and she had a big smile on her face. She hugged me and said, "Mrs. Olson, look at me! I AM somebody now!" Through tears of joy, I told her she looked amazing, but that I always knew that. I told her that clothes do not make the man, that what is in her heart is most important. We hugged again and said good-bye.

A few weeks after she was back on duty, she was killed on the Autobahn. She was buried in full dress uniform and had the traditional guards of honor. She had the American flag draped on her casket. They had the firing of volley shots as a salute to her service. There were drummers.

I am so glad that Tabatha felt she had worth before she lost her life.

A Weekend in Miami

Since I was a Child Development teacher in a large high-school, I was contacted by a textbook publisher in New York about reviewing a potential new Child Development textbook. The stipend made it appealing.

I enjoyed proofing their materials for several years, and since one thing often leads to another, I was offered an opportunity I could not refuse. The publisher was forming a small cadre of teachers from Texas, Florida, New York, Washington, and Iowa. I was asked to be Iowa's representative! The objective of the meeting was to "pick our brains about what constitutes a successful textbook". We would be flown to Miami for a weekend workshop, all expenses paid and with a stipend to boot. The publisher even paid for a substitute in the classroom so I could leave on a flight to be in Florida for a Friday evening introductory meeting.

My students were excited for me and maybe even slightly jealous. I told them I would take along their papers I needed to grade, so it was like they had a connection to Florida, too. Then off to Florida I flew.

The French Hotel where we stayed was magnificent. The price taped to the back of the door stated the daily and weekly rates. One night would have paid for a months' worth of groceries for my family of five! There was a mint on my pillowcase. The hand towels were folded in the shape of a swan. I was not in Iowa anymore!

The Friday evening session was planned as a way for all of us to get to know each other before the real work began the next morning. I was excited to meet teachers from all over the United States and to "talk shop". This was going to be a productive learning environment.

Of course, the hotel's brunch buffet the next morning was a royal treat. There was a pitcher of fresh squeezed orange juice on every table, and we could have as many glassfuls as we wanted. (I drank three. Fresh squeezed orange juice is an expensive luxury in Iowa.) There were all sorts of pastries, waffles, pancakes, cereal, eggs, bacon, sausage, rolls, and coffees, tea, and milk. And fresh squeezed orange juice, or did I mention that already? We five teachers didn't think we needed to eat again until we got to our respective homes on Sunday.

The all-day workshop was well-organized but brain-draining. None of us remembered a time in our life when we had to work so hard. Giving birth came in second! The publisher's representative, Mr. P, was very grateful that we all gave 110% that day. Our only break was for lunch. We cadre members originally said we would not be able to eat another morsel until we got home on Sunday. We forgot we had said that and stuffed ourselves again. We joked that our flight back home would require double seats.

After our last session concluded at 9 PM on Saturday night, Mr. P asked us if we all had enjoyed the experience. Then he asked if there was something he could do for us to make the experience more rewarding. I mentioned that I would have liked to have had a little down time to buy something for my children. He asked, "like what?" I told him I would like to have gotten my three kids each a Hard Rock Café T-shirt with Miami on it. He suggested going to a local Mall for one. I reminded him of the late hour, and he assured me that the Mall was still open. He got his car and we drove through heavy traffic to the Mall. When Mr. P couldn't find a close parking space, he dropped me off at the entrance to the Mall and directed me to where the Hard Rock store was and said he would meet me there in short order.

I remember watching the TV show "Miami Vice" when I was younger. In the opening of that show there were flamingoes everywhere and rats crawling around the streets. I always thought that was just for theatrics. It wasn't. It's for real! I was so caught up in watching to avoid the rats that I lost track of the direction I was headed. That's when the fear started to set in. I found no one who could understand what I was asking because no one spoke English. More fear set in. Then I spotted a couple that looked like tourists, too, so I asked them for directions to the T-shirt shop. They weren't from Miami, and they did not know where the T-shirt shop was. The FEAR was getting intense now. Suddenly someone grabbed my elbow and said "I knew afterwards that I should never have left you off alone where I did. Only then did I remember you were from Iowa and probably not used to the chaos of Miami. I'm so sorry". Mr. P had a halo over his head! He directed me to the T-shirt store where I bought three T-shirts with Miami written on them.

As we were walking back to the car, I saw a group of people standing around some sort of attraction. I asked if we could check it out; we wiggled our way right up front to see better. It was a street mime. I'd never seen a street mime before. He was wearing a shiny silver body suit, silver slippers, silver contacts, and his face and hands were painted silver. The music was techno and he was making very staccato movements. I wasn't even totally sure he was human, but rather a robot. I must have been fixated on deciding what it was I was seeing, when I felt eyes on me. Everyone in proximity was gawking at me. Mr. P said, "It's okay. She's from Iowa!"

The Sunday brunch at the hotel was even bigger than the Friday brunch. And there was a lot of fresh-squeezed orange juice again. When I checked out of the hotel the concierge gave me a red rose and a long loaf of French bread in a shopping bag as a thank you for staying with them. I boarded the airplane with my luggage, my student's ungraded papers, my rose and my French bread, and a weekend of remarkable memories.

When I arrived home and my husband met me at the airport, I was toting my rose and French bread in the shopping bag. He grinned and said, "You look like Mary Poppins!"

It was good to be back in Iowa.

The Elevator Adventure

My friend Kathy was a Spanish teacher; she and I began teaching at a large high-school in the same year and became close friends. When she asked if I would like to help chaperone some students on a weeklong trip to Mexico, I told her I would really enjoy that, but I spoke no Spanish at all; I had taken French in High-School. (My high-school French teacher was an inspiration for me to become a teacher someday.) Kathy assured me that she would teach me all the words I would need to know on the airplane.

In that airplane, 30,000 feet above the ground, I learned that "Hola meant hello", "bien meant good", "gracias meant thank-you", and "No comprende meant I don't understand". I was again assured that I would get along just fine in Mexico.

When we landed on the ground and that 30,000 feet was now above me, I realized that most of the native Mexicans liked having Americans visit because it gave them opportunities to practice their English speaking. I was going to be just fine.

My limited Spanish was put to the test in an elevator. A good-looking man and I were both going to the same floor, eight stories down. I was following all the protocol of elevators- if you are strangers, look down to the floor or at your watch or at the buttons, but avoid eye-contact at all cost. He obviously had not learned elevator protocol, because he started talking to me. He said "muy bonita". I ran through my limited new-found language and drew a blank. I then said "No comprende". He nodded his head and made an obvious and exaggerated gesture of looking me up and down, from the top of my head to my shoes. Smiling and very suggestively he said "muy bonita". I was smart (or maybe dumb) enough to know that whatever he was saying must be a compliment, so I said "gracias?". He was saying "si si" when the elevator door opened. I hurried to Kathy's room and said "muy bonita - what does it mean"? She said "why, thank you, Madelyn!" with a grin. She asked where I had learned those words. After I had told her about my elevator experience, she told me that the phrase meant "beautiful young girl".

That Spanish lesson 30,000 feet up should have included more common phrases.

I'm Feeling Lonely

Relationships and Self-Esteem are units in Health that can be sensitive to teach. Everyone has their own story to tell or not to tell. I always shared the following story to help people understand about loneliness...

My family home growing up was a drafty old farmhouse; Dad used to put rows of straw around the house in the wintertime to prevent some of the frigid winds from getting into the house. Unfortunately, animals try to seek warm places, too, and we became boarders for a family of civet cats. These creatures are related to the skunk family but have spots rather than stripes; they have the same pungent odors. The civet cats laid claim to the crawl spaces between the walls in our house. They are nocturnal animals so it was bad enough that we could hear them running through the walls at night, but their biggest problem was the awful, sulfur-smelling aroma that penetrated everything in our house. Furniture, curtains, clothing, undergarments, coats (including my mom's fur), skin, and hair-everything!!

We had no choice but to go to school smelling horrible; pretending to be sick and staying home wasn't an option because the smell made our eyes water and made breathing difficult. At least there was fresh air at school. My twin sisters, Nancy and Nadine, and I had to ride the bus to school. We were sent to the back of the bus and made to open our windows; the rest of the passengers sat up at the front of the bus near the heater. We were taunted for being stinky and gross, even by busmates who used to call us friends. At least we three had each other to commiserate with.

Getting to school created more issues. The twins had each other in their classroom; I was the only smelly person in my class. Even our best friends didn't want to claim us in that week. People stared and made faces and plugged their noses; they didn't want us to be on their study teams. No one wanted to play together at recess. I remember feeling very lonely.

Sunday brought another problem. Mom wore her warm fur coat, which had retained maximum stink. The minister asked if our family could sit in the back pew, in our own "pew"! We heard "old biddies" saying things like "why didn't they bathe before church" or even "why did they even come to church?" It was a terrible isolation.

The situation lasted for a week but seemed like forever. Eventually, after extensive research Dad found a method- the 5th one he tried- to get the uninvited guests out of our home.

That was the most infamous period of my family's lives! Being rejected and isolated for us was temporary, a quick fix. We were able to shed those feelings. How sad that there are people who have the same feelings, but they are permanent. No one, no matter what they tell you, enjoys solitude all the time.

Tale #28~

A student in my classroom was a doubting Thomas. If I showed the class something red, he would say it was green. He questioned almost everything in the textbooks. One day I was showing the class a diagram that started with two people sharing a secret; those two each told only two other people the secret; those four each told only two more people, etc. I made the comment that someone could divulge a secret at the start of the school day, and by the afternoon half of the school would have heard it.

Doubting Thomas decided to check this theory out...

At the start of his afternoon class, I told Doubting Thomas I was surprised to see him. He asked what I meant. I told him that I heard he was in a car accident in the parking lot that morning and that he was badly hurt. "Really, what else did you hear?" he asked. I gave him more detail: it wasn't his fault, his parents' car was totaled, and he was taken to a local hospital.

Doubting Thomas said, "Dang, that chart was right! I made everything up and started the rumor myself." I wanted to say, "I told you so", but I refrained...

Tale #29~

We were in a unit in Child Development that explained the four ways people grow: physically, mentally, socially, and emotionally. We were discussing how the growth was not equilateral and was not at the same rate for all persons. I shared an example of my arm strength; because I use my arm and hand strength to decorate wedding cakes, I had damage in my carpal tunnels and required surgery. When the doctor measured the pre-surgery strength, he was amazed that my numbers were better than most people's post-surgery strength. I commented to the students that I could still arm wrestle and be a good competitor. Charlie, always good for a dare, said "I bet you can't beat me!" I told him that if he got at least a "B" in class, I would take him up on the challenge on the last day of class.

Months went by and Charlie worked hard to get and maintain a "B" in class. I thought he might have forgotten our deal. The last day of class Charlie ran into the classroom and said, "I'm ready to beat you at arm wrestling, Mrs. Olson". He arranged the desks so we could be observed by the whole class. With his size and youthfulness, he didn't entertain losing in front of his peers. It was a good fight, but, lose he did. He ran out of the room as fast as he had run in. Never dare a woman with strength on her side!

Tale #30~

As a cheerleading sponsor, one of my duties was driving the cheer-leaders to out-of-town games. We were headed home after a victorious ballgame when I could hear the girls whispering in the back seat of the car. When we got to a stoplight at a not-so-busy intersection, the girls all jumped out of the car and took their place in front of the headlights. Then they each dropped their Lolli and wiggled their little rear ends, laughing the whole time. I quickly pushed the "lock" button on all the doors and slowly drove off. I could see the girls tugging to pull up their panties as they were running after the car. They were yelling, "Please Mrs. Olson, we will never do that again!" I stopped the car and said "You are right. You will not." I was glad the interior of the car was dark so the girls could not see the mirth on my face.

Tale #31~

There are some career paths in which an absence just means that your work will still be there when you get back. That is not true in the teaching field. An absence means that sub plans need to be made, including classroom procedures and details about discipline. Sometimes it's easier to come to school sicker than a dog, than to pull yourself out of the sick bed to make detailed lesson plans.

I was preparing to be absent because I was going to be presenting an in-service out of town the next day. I just knew that my plans had covered all the bases for my classes- any sub would be able to sub in my classroom. I wasn't even going to worry about it!

The unit was anatomy. The substitute was a retired former elementary teacher. When I returned the following day and asked my students if they had any questions about the material that had been covered by the sub, they all started laughing. I learned that the sub was uncomfortable saying the correct terminology for the male anatomy. An astute male in the back row noticed that she dropped her pencil and knelt behind the podium at the same time she named one of the body parts. So, he asked her to repeat the term. Again, her delivery was: 1) drop the pencil, 2) hide behind the podium, and 3) say the term.

I asked the students how many times she dropped her pencil. In unison, they said "5 times"!

The best laid plans always have a flaw in them!

Tale #32~

Textbooks often include superfluous information. I had used a chapter in a Foods and Nutrition textbook to prepare a lesson for my class on "formal dining". One of the sections in that chapter was on writing a menu in the correct formal format. It required listing the foods in the order in which they are consumed and center-justifying the list. I demonstrated the technique, but not without having trouble with the latter. Thank goodness I could erase and try again on the chalkboard. The students would not have that same luxury as they would be using ink pens on paper. A student raised her hand and asked, "why do we need to learn this? My Mom never has, and she's old!" I thought for a minute, ripped up the instructions, threw them over my shoulder, and said "you're right! I've never had to use it either, nor did my Mom, and she's really old!"

Tale #33~

As a teacher I want the students in my class to be studious. I always want them to be eager learners, good listeners, meticulous note-takers, team players, and effective articulators- all with a smile.

From time to time, a student on a teacher's roster "marches to the beat of a different drum". Robert had a drum that was too massive to fit through my classroom door! He listened well, never interrupting or asking questions, but he maintained that he did not need to take notes, so he sat quietly while everyone else took copious notes. Nothing I said or did could convince him to put his pencil to the paper. I told him I was concerned that he would have no notes with which to study prior to test-taking. He would tap his head and say, "it's all up here".

I made a deal with Robert. I told him that if he could get at least a B on the first test, without using anyone else's notes, I would not require him to take notes for the rest of the semester. If he got less than a B, he would need to take notes for the rest of the semester. He whole-heartedly agreed and we shook hands.

He took less time than any other student to complete the first test. I just knew that he wasn't getting the information from his brain to the test form, otherwise he would have required more time, right?

Robert got the highest grade in the class with a perfect 100%.

For the rest of the semester he listened well, never interrupting or asking questions, and sat quietly while everyone else took copious notes. He aced every test. Every. One. Of them. Some students march to the beat of a different drum and produce an amazing melody.

Tale #34~

Music can create a relaxing environment. Learning takes place in a relaxed environment. But the music needs to be relaxing itself, like classical music, or smooth instrumentals, not heavy metal or techno-type sounds.

Sara, our firstborn, entered High-School in 1983. This was the time before personal computers or earbuds. She had a portable radio that was her means of creating a learning environment, and her favorite music was loud and peppy songs like "Wake Me Up Before You Go, Girl" or "Eye of the Tiger" or "Let's Hear it for the Boy". I mentioned to her that the music was going to interfere with her concentration. She disagreed and said it had the opposite effect on her. Rather than arguing the point

I said that her first grade reports would be the proof in the pudding. Her first report card showed all A's. In fact, every quarter for four years she got straight A's.

Sara was one of two Valedictorians in a class of 250 students. She surely enjoyed her music!

Tale #35~

Sometimes a child can be the teacher and the parent can be the learner. Our son Jay had a truck with a lift kit on it which meant that it nearly required a ladder for a short passenger to take their seat in the cab. I am short and I required some assistance to get into his truck. Jay had taken his position behind the wheel, but we were not moving yet. Jay just kept looking at me and finally said, "Put your seatbelt on, Mom." Now, I had grown up before seatbelts and was still alive and well to talk about it, so I balked at wearing a seatbelt. I pouted and said, "Nope, and you can't make me!" Again, he said, "Put your seatbelt on, Mom." I responded "No, it wrinkles my clothes". He said, "Put your seatbelt on, Mom." I said "No, the seatbelt rubs on my neck." He said, "Put your seatbelt on, Mom." I said, "No, it smushes my girlie parts." Then he said, "Put your seatbelt on, Mom. I love you and don't want you to die." I couldn't get my seatbelt on fast enough...

Tale #36~

Nursing home residents enjoy visits from children and young adults. My Health II students had just finished a unit on "Aging", so I arranged to take them to a local nursing home to interact with senior citizens. The students worked in pairs as they asked their assigned senior citizen questions about their growing up years. With the information they gathered, they wrote about their new elderly friend's life and then presented the booklets at a second visit to the nursing home.

There was an odd number of students in my class, so B.K and I paired off to interview an elderly retired farmer who was appropriately donned in bib overalls. He seemed pleased to be getting attention as he shared stories of his youth, and B.K. and I enjoyed learning about his life. He was right in the middle of a sentence when his head dropped to his chest, and B.K. and I looked at each other with horror on our faces; we were sure our new friend had just died right before our very eyes! After what seemed like an eternity, he raised his head and he continued his sentence exactly where he had left off! An attending nurse must have seen our puzzled looks because she came to our table and quietly whispered in my ear that the gentleman farmer had narcolepsy! When the same event happened several more times during our interview, at least we were prepared.

One of the senior citizens was a retired teacher; she corrected the grammar in the booklet presented to her!

We learned later that one family chose to have the booklet read at the funeral of their parent.

Many of my students were saddened when they saw their new friends name in the obituary section of the local newspaper.

Friends come in all ages...

Janey's Journey

I would be remiss if I didn't share the story of Janey.

Janey was born into a family of tall, stately people. She was the baby of the family who moved to our town from out-of-state after most of her siblings had graduated from high school and/or college. Janey's father worked at a nearby farm equipment dealership and raised a few horses on their acreage. He and his attractive wife modeled respect and strong family values to their large family.

When I first met Janey, her life had already been altered. As a young child she was horse-back riding with a friend when, in her own words, she was "showing off her riding skills" and she and the horse both landed on the ground. The weight and impact of the horse on a young body caused extensive physical and neurological damage. After extensive medical attention, in addition to stunting her growth, Janey does not have total control of the left side of her body: her left eye (now sewn shut)tears constantly, the left side of her mouth droops so she has a lop-sided smile, she lacks feeling on the left side of her face so eating is difficult, she has a stagger to her walk; because of the lack of feeling in her extremities, she often walks right out of her slip-on shoes.

The first time I met Janey, I loved her! In that first year of friendship, she hung out in our office area in her free time, offering to help us with any tasks we needed to complete. In her next three years of high school she built her class schedules around my prep time and lunchtime, so we could be together. She appointed herself my private secretary. She kept our office area organized, she helped make bulletin boards, she retrieved our mail, she sorted out papers to save time in the classroom, she took phone messages for us. We could not and would not have wanted to survive without her help. Janey made my teaching life easier!

Janey was a student in several of my classes over those four years. In one of the classes, I was teaching a unit on the importance of healthy self-esteem. I had asked the students if anyone would like to share an instance in their life when someone "moved mountains for them" by bestowing them with a genuine compliment. As I looked around the room waiting for what I anticipated would be multiple stories, a lone hand went up. It was Janey. All eyes were on her, some curious to see what she might offer. She humbly shared her story. Then she framed her face with her hands and said, "My Mom says I'm beautiful, even though I look like this." A tear escaped her left eye; tears escaped both of my eyes. I said that her Mom was "absolutely correct", and that beauty comes from within a person. She was truly the most beautiful person in that classroom!

It has been more than 30 years since Janey graced our classrooms and office. In every year since then I have received a Christmas card, an anniversary card, and a birthday card from Janey and her mom. I am so glad I was a part of Janey's journey.

Looking in the Rearview Mirror

There have been a lot of changes in schools since the earth cooled for me.

Computers were not even part of my vocabulary when I began teaching, and now in many schools every student has his or her own personal computer.

The students also have cell phones, although I'm just old-school enough to think they are more of a distractor than an asset in the classroom.

I used to make my own multiple mimeographed copies, collated them by hand, and stapled them so they were class ready. Now a stream-lined piece of equipment can make hundreds of copies at a time, front and back, collated, 3-hole punched, and stapled in a matter of minutes. However, I admit I did like the smell of the mimeographed handouts!

The microwave oven had not yet been mass-produced for the family kitchens when I began teaching Home-Economics. I remember when a representative of a local appliance center brought a demo to class; it was bulky, and it had a wire-mesh screen that was part of the door. The representative showed us how this miracle machine operated. All the students were in awe! When they asked if you could cook a hard-boiled egg in it, the gentleman said he didn't know for sure, but he thought we could try one. In short order the egg blew up and forced tiny particles of eggs into the wire mesh. He said, "In answer to your question, the answer is definitely NO". Today the microwave is utilized more than most appliances in our kitchens.

People have asked me if I would still want to be a teacher if I could start all over again. There is no doubt in my mind that I chose the right field for me! I know things are different now. I know students are different now; when I was young if a person of authority told me to jump, I would have said, "yes sir, how high". A few students today tell the teacher where to jump. Most of today's students still have the same goals and hopes and fears and ambitions as did my generation. Yes, I would do it all over again. How else would I have met thousands of students who have helped me make enough memories to last for a lifetime.

To have an impact on generations to come there are three things you should do: plant a tree, have a child, and write a book. Now I can put a big red checkmark by all three items.

CPSIA information can be obtained
at www.ICGtesting.com
Printed in the USA
LVHW080340090521
686901LV00017B/862